SIN: A GUIDE FOR THE PERPLEXED

T&T Clark *Guides for the Perplexed*

T&T Clark's Guides for the Perplexed are clear, concise, and accessible introductions to thinkers, writers, and subjects that students and readers can find especially challenging. Concentrating specifically on what it is that makes the subject difficult to grasp, these books explain and explore key themes and ideas, guiding the reader toward a thorough understanding of demanding material.

Guides for the Perplexed **available from T&T Clark:**

De Lubac: A Guide for the Perplexed, David Grumett
Christian Bioethics: A Guide for the Perplexed, Agneta Sutton
Calvin: A Guide for the Perplexed, Paul Helm
Tillich: A Guide for the Perplexed, Andrew O'Neill
The Trinity: A Guide for the Perplexed, Paul M. Collins
Christology: A Guide for the Perplexed, Alan Spence
Wesley: A Guide for the Perplexed, Jason E. Vickers
Pannenberg: A Guide for the Perplexed, Timothy Bradshaw
Balthasar: A Guide for the Perplexed, Rodney Howsare
Theological Anthropology: A Guide for the Perplexed, Marc Cortez
Benedict XVI: A Guide for the Perplexed, Tracey Rowland
Eucharist: A Guide for the Perplexed, Ralph N. McMichael
Process Theology: A Guide for the Perplexed, Bruce Epperly

Forthcoming Titles:

Political Theology: A Guide for the Perplexed, Elizabeth Philips
Martyrdom: A Guide for the Perplexed, Paul Middleton

SIN: A GUIDE
FOR THE PERPLEXED

DEREK R. NELSON

t & t clark

Published by T&T Clark International
A Continuum Imprint
The Tower Building, 11 York Road, London SE1 7NX
80 Maiden Lane, Suite 704, New York, NY 10038

www.continuumbooks.com

British Library Cataloguing-in-Publication Data
A catalogue record for this book is available from the British Library

ISBN13 :   978-0-567-64367-4 (Hardback)
           978-0-567-54275-5 (Paperback)

Typeset by Newgen Imaging Systems Pvt Ltd, Chennai, India
Printed and bound in Great Britain

For Kelly

CONTENTS

ACKNOWLEDGMENTS

Writing on sin as I have for several years now, I have incurred several debts that I cannot hope to repay. The first debts are to many teachers from whose guidance I have benefitted in thinking through problems in theological understandings of creation and human nature. Here I must mention at least the names of David Kelsey, Miroslav Volf, the late William Placher, Stephen Webb, Ted Peters, and the late Timothy Lull. Richard Schenk, OP, encouraged me to press the "gnesio-Lutheran" seriousness of sin into the contemporary theological agenda. Though he did not make a Flacian of me, he did come close, and I am very grateful for his support. Most people would count themselves lucky to have studied with just a couple from the above group. That I can count them all teachers and friends is a great gift.

For the last 4 years I have called Thiel College home, and many colleagues here have richly contributed to my thinking on these matters. I am especially grateful for the commitment to interdisciplinarity that infuses scholarship and teaching at Thiel. Such a widening of perspectives has made me into a theologian who does not shrink from natural or social scientific approaches to theological questions, and who sees as one of his "publics" the wider academic community for whom particular theological commitments have neither intellectual weight nor existential import. Curtis L. Thompson read an entire draft of this text, and I have greatly benefitted from his insights. Bryan Wagoner has been an important theological conversation partner for many years now. The New Testament scholar George Branch-Trevathan helped enormously in thinking through issues as broad as "Paul on sin" and as narrow as the proper pointing of Hebrew verbs. Others in Greenville, such as Martin Roth (from whose gift of portions of his personal library much of my reading has come), Sean McConnor, and the sagacious Seth Myers are also to be thanked as is Larry Lyke.

Portions of this text were written with the support of the Northwestern Pennsylvania Synod of the Evangelical Lutheran Church in America, and I am glad to thank them, and Bishop Ralph Jones, for their support. During the writing of this book I also worked closely in pastoral ministry with the Rev. Albert Gesler, Jr., Tammy Williams, and Heather Wilt, and I appreciate their cooperation and good humor more than I can say. I would also like to thank Thomas Kraft and his many gifted colleagues at T&T Clark/Continuum. To work with them really has been a pleasure.

Last, the personal debts are always among the most difficult to properly name, though I feel them most keenly. I apologize here in print to the students at Thiel and elsewhere whose wait-time for returned tests and papers increased significantly during the writing of this text. For the parishioners at Twelve Apostles Lutheran Church in Saegertown, PA, and at Holy Trinity Lutheran Church, Greenville, PA, I am grateful, especially as they listened to more sermons about sin than most folks have since Edwards was preaching.

Finally, I owe so very much to my wife Kelly, in large part due to the fact that she would say I don't owe her anything at all. Though I'm certain this is one of the odder things a man has given his wife, and that she can't possibly want it, this book is nonetheless for her.

ABBREVIATIONS

Adv. haer.	Irenaeus of Lyons, *Against Heresies*
CD	Karl Barth, *Church Dogmatics*
C. Iul.	Augustine, *Against Julian*
Conf.	Augustine, *Confessions*
De civ. Dei.	Augustine, *City of God*
De corr. et gr.	Augustine, *On Rebuke and Grace*
De Gen. ad litt.	Augustine, *On the Literal Meaning of Genesis*
De lib. arb	Augustine, *On Free Will*
De mor. eccl. cath.	Augustine, *On the Morals of the Catholic Church*
De pecc. mer. et remiss.	Augustine, *On Merit and the Forgiveness of Sins*
De nupt. et conc.	Augustine, *On Marriage and Concupiscence*
De trin.	Augustine, *On the Trinity*
LW	Martin Luther, *Luther's Works*
Retr.	Augustine, *Retractions*
Ser.	Augustine, *Sermons*
Sel. in Ex.	Origen, *Selected Homilies on Genesis and Exodus*
WA	Martin Luther, *Weimar Ausgabe* (Collected Works)

CHAPTER 1

THE GOOD NEWS ABOUT SIN

Whenever I have to choose between two evils, I always like to try the one I haven't tried before.

—*Mae West*

The worst sin toward our fellow creatures is not to hate them, but to be indifferent to them; that's the essence of inhumanity.

—*George Bernard Shaw*

Tout comprendre, c'est tout pardonner. (To understand everything is to forgive everything.)

—*French Proverb*

This book is entitled *Sin: A Guide for the Perplexed*. I therefore need to establish at the outset that I am firmly in favor of both sin and perplexity. How can I mean this? As will become clear throughout the book, I am of the opinion that invoking the language of sin to account for the misery and evil experienced in the world bears in its wake both explanatory force and reason for hope that other alternative vocabularies do not and cannot offer.[1] Sin has, built into it, a kind of good news. Perplexity about sin and evil, too, is good news. It is a tendency of humans to try to explain sin and evil in such ways that they make sense, or fit in, to our world of thought. Such attempts are not only often callow and misleading; they also "do the devil a favor," to paraphrase Søren Kierkegaard, by *hiding* the profoundly God-negating character of evil.[2] Attempts to reconcile the being of God with the being of evil are called theodicies, and I intend to argue against them. Most theodicies issue in a kind of rhetorical tone deafness to real human suffering. People who live through terrible tragedy, or a life of misery and suffering, should not have to hear that God has used their suffering for some other end, no matter how good that end is. God does not merely instrumentalize sin and evil; a basic premise of Christianity has been that God defeats it.[3]

Those, like the great philosopher Gottfried Leibniz (1646–1716), who intend to assuage the pain of suffering by pointing out the final powerlessness of evil, do just the opposite. One theologian who cannot be accused of not taking sin seriously enough, Karl Barth (1886–1968), writes of such an approach, "But how faint and easily misheard is this echo when the reference is to a powerless nothing which God cannot fight and overcome as a real enemy! How trite and trivial is that which in the New Testament is not at all self-evident but a costly reality and truth."[4] Better to insist that sin and evil stand directly against God's intentions, contrary to God's will, rather than to try to explain how evil fits into the grand scheme of redemption and creation. The edges of what we experience as sin and evil ought to be honed, not dulled.

Therefore, remaining perplexed about sin has much to commend as an approach. Those who know the rough contours of evil can better resist them and are more aware of their contrasts with the goodness of creation. But perplexity about the thing itself and clarity about how the thing has been described are not mutually exclusive. It is in that vein, and toward that end, that this book is directed. Perplexity at sin, yes. Perplexity at the doctrine of sin, no.

What is the good news about sin? Sin, as opposed to philosophical theories, scientific explanations, or other humanistic approaches to the question of human wickedness and evil, introduces God as an element in the violation. To use the language of sin to account for moral fault has the benefit of invoking the violation not just of transcendent norms, but of transcendence itself. And when transcendence itself is understood to be ingredient in the experience of moral failure and ethical rupture, then the healing and reconciliatory aid of transcendence itself becomes suddenly available. The good news about sin is—must it be said?—forgiveness.[5] Sin is not simply a pious name given to naughty acts that harm others. To say that an action is sinful is to get God deeply involved. In the middle ages, a common distinction was used by moral philosophers to differentiate between different kinds of "bad" acts according to the recipient of offense. An act was *criminal* if it was an offense to the state, it was *immoral* if it was an offense to another person, and it was *sinful* if it was an offense to God. Many actions were, of course, offenses to all three. One thinks of murder, say, as an example of something that is criminal, immoral, and sinful. Some actions might have been only criminal, and neither immoral nor sinful. Driving 35 miles per hour in a 30 mile-an-hour zone, for example, is not ordinarily thought of as being immoral, since no one in particular is necessarily harmed by the action. It is also not sinful, since the decision to make that particular stretch of road a 30 mph zone instead of a 40 mph zone is a (more or less) arbitrary human decision. Conversely, some acts which we think of as being "sinful" might be neither criminal nor immoral. Viewing pornography, for example, is sometimes said to be a victimless act, but it nonetheless may be seen to contradict, say, God's intentions for the gift of sexuality. One would have to confess a sin to a priest (that is, if staying with our middle ages scenario), but not acts that were strictly criminal or unethical.[6] In fact, criminal or unethical acts could not be easily "atoned" for at all. The grace of forgiveness washed away the guilt of sin, but left the criminal on his own.

Therefore, sin is good news. In the words of Stephen Webb, "The stronger your sense of sin . . . the clearer your understanding of grace . . . Sin is not only a great leveler but also a necessary motivator—and these two sides of the doctrine of sin fit snugly together. Sin frees us from the anxiety of trying to be perfect, as well as the burden of saving the world." For those who are uninterested in saving the world, knowing that it is already saved, the word of sin is utterly freeing, as grace is its presupposition. "Liberated from utopian fantasies and confronted with our basic human solidarity, we can serve others while being humble about our accomplishments and realistic about the possibilities for personal improvement and social change."[7] The goodness of God makes sin possible, in a sense, but the goodness of forgiveness makes sin relative, penultimate, and soon to be defeated.

OBJECTIONS AND HANG-UPS: WHY SIN OFFENDS US

Sin might be making a comeback.[8] But if it is, it is only because it had been relegated to the darker corners of Christianity. The doctrine of sin seems to have fallen into relative disrepute over the last few decades.[9] Though its status as a central doctrine of the Christian faith was not seriously challenged by professional churchly theologians, and though the vocabulary of sin was not altogether abandoned by laypersons seeking to make sense of the moral life, nonetheless people like the famed psychologist Karl Menninger were moved to wonder "Whatever Became of Sin?"[10] An empirical demonstration of the "eclipse" of sin-talk would be virtually impossible. Yet consider the following data. The hymnals of several major Protestant denominations for centuries used to have a section heading for hymns about "sin." None do so any longer. Virtually every Protestant and Roman Catholic liturgy that began with a confession spoke openly and plainly about "sin" as the reason necessitating confession. This is no longer universally the case.[11] The self-esteem movement has become so axiomatic in our child rearing that numerous children's Bibles have opted to omit the story of the "fall" of Adam and Eve. To talk with children about sin is potentially to make them feel bad about themselves, which is profoundly offensive to current patterns of parenting. For these and a whole host of other reasons, some trivial and some weighty, it has become unfashionable in many circles of contemporary Christianity to talk seriously about sin. William James noted a century ago, "We have now whole congregations, whose preachers, far from magnifying our consciousness of sin, seem devoted rather to making little of it."[12] Let us consider a few of the major reasons *why* the pattern of proclaiming the Christian gospel as the response to sin has been eclipsed by a variety of replacements. The list is intended to be illustrative rather than exhaustive; many more reasons could surely be given for sin's eclipse. Here we look at four typical objections to the language of sin as an orienting perspective in Christian theology.

Objection 1: Pessimism

Christian doctrines of sin appear to some as bearing all the marks of a defeatist, pessimistic attitude that undercuts efforts at moral progress, justifies minimalistic exertion in the pursuit of love and justice, and obviates attempts at change in the moral order. If sin is all-pervasive and ineradicable this side of the eschaton, after all, and a world that does not include it cannot be imagined, what purpose would there be in trying to escape its clutches? According to this kind of logic, a doctrine of sin is the best friend of a wicked status quo. Richard Dawkins, who has contributed to a little cottage industry based on not understanding, and yet vehemently denouncing, Christian commitments, typifies this concern that an emphasis on sin erodes moral commitment. "The Christian focus is overwhelmingly on sin sin sin

4

sin sin sin sin. What a nasty little preoccupation to have running your life."[13] According to Dawkins's way of thinking, someone who already has sin on the mind will either feel lousy about oneself and thus not try not to sin, or will be so focused on salacious and prurient pursuits that further sinning becomes inevitable.

The great poet Alexander Pope came to a similar conclusion, but on much different grounds. In his remarkable poem *An Essay on Man*, Pope writes, "Vice is a monster of such frightful mien / As to be hated needs but to be seen. / Yet seen too oft, familiar with her face, / We first endure, then pity, then embrace."[14] If we keep sin, and thus sin-talk, at an arm's length, it will seem foreign, forbidden, and thus perhaps unappealing. But focusing on it too much leads eventually to its embrace. The logical thing to do, according to this objection, is to limit the attention one pays to sin, and to find a different way of speaking about human moral possibilities. And yet it seems clear that simply complaining that it is unpleasant to believe in sin is not an argument with any force. If it made a distasteful thing less likely to exist by asserting that one did not believe in it, work would begin immediately to have all people announce that they did not believe in cancer, abuse, and addiction. The objection that sin thus is overly pessimistic about human nature, though frequently leveled, seems finally unsatisfying.

Objection 2: Arbitrariness

Whatever else we desire when it comes to moral direction, one constant attribute that we tend to desire is uniformity. Or put into other words, we desire consistency. When one child is treated a certain way by a parent, and another is not, our basic sense of justice is violated. When one action is not allowed by a parent for a long time, and suddenly the action is permitted, our sense of the durability of justice is dishonored. Further, the basic authority of the parent is eroded when changes to what are considered allowed or disallowed actions are arbitrarily made.

A basic teaching of Christian theology is that God's will does not change. Since his word does not change, principles of right and wrong do not change, and thus what counts as a sin should not change. Little wonder, then, that when church bodies overturn denunciations of certain practices as "sinful," their members are frequently outraged, or at least upset. Eating meat on Fridays was, for centuries, contrary to the will of God according to Roman Catholic teaching. Likewise, if a woman did not wear a veil during a church worship service, this was considered, for many centuries, to be a sin. Usury—the practice of lending money and collecting interest—was condemned by the church for a very long time. It has, of course, become practically expected in Christian countries that capitalism, and the lending practices that underwrite and advance it, will be the economic norm. Slavery was approved by very many Christian churches until relatively recently. The Vatican itself condoned slavery as at least potentially "natural" until well into the nineteenth century. It now views such a social institution as profoundly sinful.[15] Changing views on limbo, that place to which the unbaptized but virtuous pagans might be eternally consigned, also causes people to question the continuity of teaching on the topic of sin. Thus the force of this second objection would be that language about sin must either be essentially static, and thus unable to respond to a changing world, or else adaptable to current needs, and thus somehow less than timelessly authoritative.

Objection 3: Inapplicability

A third objection has been that language of sin is hopelessly out of date, and therefore, while potentially quaint, not really applicable to contemporary faith and life. After all, such an objection might say, among the things denounced as sins in the Old Testament are football, cheeseburgers, and allowing people of other faiths to live. "Touching the skin of a pig" is forbidden in Lev. 11.6–8, which rules out American football as long as the ball is made of pigskin. "Mixing dairy products and meat products" has been understood to be forbidden in Deut. 14.21, Exod. 23.19, and Exod. 34.26. And Deut. 13.6–10 enjoins murdering anyone who worships other gods, as they may try to lure one of the chosen people away from the worship of the one true God. Of course, critics of Christianity (and Judaism) have made a sport of ridiculing such moral beliefs, and indeed have taken them completely out of context and ignored extenuating circumstances in so doing. Nonetheless, it seems perfectly reasonable to wonder whether a tradition that at least seems to condemn activities we have come to see as perfectly normal and morally appropriate (football, cheeseburgers, and freedom of religion) is too out of step with our world to make any sense. Though it may raise some eyebrows to do so, a discussion of the sin of masturbation may illumine how many people have objected to sin-talk as inapplicable to their daily lives.

The act of masturbation is, according to official Catholic church teaching, sinful. Many people have had a laugh at this seemingly antiquated teaching, not least of all the British comedy troupe Monty Python. In the film *The Meaning of Life*, a man who has fathered dozens of children cheerily leads in singing the song "Every Sperm Is Sacred." The lyrics of the song lampoon, but perhaps do not really misrepresent, the official Catholic position. Lines from the chorus include: "Every sperm is sacred. Every sperm is great; if a sperm is wasted, God gets quite irate." The logic of the position goes something like this: in order for sexual intercourse to conform to the purposes for which God intended it, three conditions must apply. First, the couple must be married. Second, the purpose of the sexual intercourse must be procreation. Third, the act is to be "unitive" in the sense that a bond forms between the sex partners. The only kind of act that is unitive, procreative, and marital is genital-genital intercourse between husband and wife. All other sexual contact is inappropriate, immoral, and sinful. Which places this sexual ethic far from the mainstream understanding of many people living in the modern world.

Frequently the story of Onan, in Genesis 38, is cited as evidence for the sinfulness of masturbation. Onan's brother Er died, leaving a widow, Tamar, but no children. Judah, the father of Onan and Er, directed Onan to take Tamar as his own wife and to produce children with her. Onan was reluctant to do so, since the children would not be considered his, and so each time he had sexual relations with Tamar, he performed *coitus interruptus* and, as the King James Version states, "spilled his seed on the ground" (Gen. 38.9). God is displeased with this habit and strikes Onan down dead on the spot. Though this is obviously not a case of private self-gratification, as masturbation is usually considered to be, many theological commentators have understood the vain wasting of semen, generally, to incur God's displeasure. Let the third century Christian theologian Clement of Alexandria be our exemplar here. Clement influentially stated, "To indulge in intercourse without intending children is to outrage nature, which we should take as our instructor."[16] Clement actually felt—and he was not alone in this in the early church—that desire as such was evil. He thought that a married man ought so to practice continence that when he engaged in sexual intercourse with his wife, he did so not desiring *her*, but desiring that the act itself would produce offspring.[17] Indeed, as Clement put it, "To have sex for any reason other than the procreation of children is to harm nature."[18]

How does this apply in our life and time? It does, on the face of it, seem to be quite out of step with what the rest of the culture assumes and teaches. We might ask the same questions of sex before marriage; some object to calling premarital sexual relations a sin. They argue that monogamous sexual activity only within the bounds of marriage was articulated as an ethical norm (and its violation a sin) in cultures in which young people married very soon after reaching puberty. It is one thing to ask a young woman or man to remain chaste outside of marriage until the age of 15, when they might well be married. But it is quite another to insist that a young person remain chaste in modern Western culture, where the average age of first marriages in, for example, the United Kingdom is 30.7 for men and 28.5 for women, in Spain is 33.6 for men and 32.9 for women, and in Japan is 35 for men and 27.5 for women.[19] If the average age of puberty in boys is 12, then the average Japanese Roman Catholic man will be expected to remain chaste for 23 years. This hardly seems in line with the intentions and assumptions of biblical writers. Thus, the objection that definitions of sin are arbitrary seems to carry some force.

Objection 4: Appearing judgmental

In the lexicon of vices of the modern day, one that stands out for particular censure is appearing to be judgmental. To declare some actions "sins" and others "permissible" is to presume too much, some object. One of the worst things one can be called is "judgmental." Of course, there are forms of judgment which are pernicious, capricious, and presumptuous. But such impudence is certainly different from rendering *genuine judgment*. When the knowable facts of a case are not given due attention and a decision is reached, then judgment has not been genuine. When a person's opposing viewpoint is not fully appreciated (in the sense of Iamblichus's *dissoi logoi*)[20] before a conclusion is pronounced, then judgment has not been genuine. And so being "judgmental" in this sense is certainly a problem. Yet it is neither rational nor healthy to hold beliefs that one does not believe to be true, and when such beliefs imply that their opposites are false, it is neither rational nor healthy to pretend that no such conflict on a given matter exists, and thus that judgment not be rendered. This does not mean that undue attention should be focused on exposing the sins of others, nor that the faults of oneself should not be considered before rendering any kind of judgment (cf. Mt. 7.1, Rom. 2.1, 14.4, Jas. 4.11–12). But judgment itself is no vice, and avoiding rendering it at all costs is no real objection to talk about sin.

SIN'S CONTRARIES

Sin is good news because it requires that language of God reenter discussions of moral fault, evil, and suffering. As discussed above, sin is primarily *against God*. Alisdair MacIntyre, in trying to differentiate between a theological account of virtue given by Peter Abelard and a philosophical one from Aristotle, writes, "What Christianity requires is a conception not merely of defects of character, or vices, but of breaches of divine laws, of sin."[21] In other words, the value added by theological discourse is in identifying a role for God in the experience of human misery and evil. Sin is good news because it is against God.

But in what sense is it against him? That is not as easy a question to answer as it might first appear. In fact, as understandings of sin have developed over centuries, the answers given to that question (though admittedly the question has rarely been asked directly) vary quite widely. All major Christian theologians agree that sin is somehow against God. But what does it mean to say that something is "against" anything or anyone else? Let us take a brief tour of the understandings of sin of three major theologians, each with a different idea of sin's contrary. We begin with Anselm of Canterbury (1033–1109), who conceived of the contrary of sin as the *honor of God*, then move to John Calvin (1509–64), who conceived of the contrary of sin as the *law of God*, and end with Martin Luther (1483–1546), for whom the contrary of sin is the *word of God*. The purpose of this exercise is not merely to become clearer on these three theologians' notions of sin (though such an understanding may be gleaned, free of charge), but rather to highlight the many possibilities for construing sin's against-ness.

Sin as offense against God's honor

"Honor" is an easy-to-know, but hard-to-define concept. When one has been shamed, one knows the loss of honor in a direct, noncognitive way.

Honor, one might say, is the name we give to the correspondence of intrinsic worth and recognized worth. In other words, honor is shown when the estimation one has of the worth of some other is in accord with the actual worth of that other. I honor a pet dog when I feed it, since it is worthy of my care and respect, but I dishonor a child when I spend more resources on the dog than the child, the child's "worth" being greater. To take the point further, the dog is also dishonored when it is treated as the equivalent of a child, since it is incapable of supplying the kind of reciprocal relationship its owner desires. As a minister, I have a particular responsibility to honor the one whom I eulogize at a funeral. To heap up one-sided, hagiographic praise upon, or to denounce in ceaseless detail, the life of the deceased are equally dishonoring. Honor requires knowing, and telling, the truth.[22]

One medieval thinker who has exercised considerable influence over the way Christians in the West have thought about atonement, and therefore, derivatively, sin, is Anselm of Canterbury. Anselm conceived of sin as a debt owed to God by humanity. In order for the debt to be canceled, someone had to pay the penalty owed God. The penalty was infinite, because the sin had inflicted infinite damage. The damage is to God's *honor*. A sin is any act that has not been fully subjugated to the will of God.[23] When a moral agent commits a sin, he dishonors God. Anselm writes, "To sin is not to render one's due to God."[24] Language of "due" and "honor" shows how Anselm's theological framework is dependent on the cultures around him—the culture of the monastery and the culture of the feudal manor. The monastic world where Anselm made his home was thought to be a kind of microcosm of the order that lies at the heart of God, and the same hierarchy ordered the political life of feudal Europe. Kings ruled vassals, lords ruled serfs, abbots ruled novices, and so on. When a member of a lower station wronged a member of a higher station, the dishonor thereby caused—and therefore, the debt thereby incurred—was greater than when a greater wronged a lesser. A female serf who disrespected the manor lord's honor brought more shame than a male serf's disrespect, for example. Crimes committed in a given lord's town were not just seen as disturbing the peace there. Rather, they were signs of disrespect for the lord himself.

Though times have certainly changed from medieval feudalism, this notion still connects with the modern mind. Speaking as a professor, for example, when a student plagiarizes in one of my classes, the harm done is not only to the dignity of scholarship as such, or the system of rights and wrongs that governs it. I feel personally betrayed. It seems as though the student has such little regard for my teaching office that such an action would be deemed permissible. One's honor is existentially close to one's heart. If it is violated, the harm done to the one dishonored needs to be offset. Since the worth of the one dishonored is not itself affected by the dishonor undergone, and since the worth of the one who dishonors is not affected, all that remains possible is for the dishonored to return a correspondingly low "estimation" of the worth of the one who dishonors.

At the time of this writing, Elin Nordegren, ex-wife of professional golfer Tiger Woods, is set to auction off millions of dollars of jewelry given to her by her former husband. Ms. Nordegren felt publicly humiliated and dishonored as reports of her husband's numerous infidelities spread. A natural course of action to take, in such a case, is to inflict some kind of richly symbolic dishonor back onto the offender. By selling off the jewelry he purchased (done in large part, she feels, to hide his embarrassment over indiscretions and to "atone" for harms done), Nordegren has thus righted the scales of justice and honor by showing her correspondingly low estimation of Woods's gifts and the very person whose love they were supposed to betoken.

To Anselm's medieval way of thinking, the offense done to someone who is dishonored is greater when the one who dishonors is of a lower station. When this logic is taken as a model for the dishonor incurred by God in sin, the debt incurred rises exponentially, even infinitely. No matter how high the station of the sinner is, and no matter how slight the grievance, when the dishonor is done to God the debt becomes infinite. As Anselm himself puts it, "This is the debt which angels and men owe to God. No one who pays it sins; everyone who does not pay it sins. This is the sole and entire honor which we owe to God, and God requires from us. One who does not render this honor to God takes away from God what belongs to him, and dishonors God, and to do this is to sin. Moreover, as long as he does not repay what he has stolen, he remains at fault."[25] Honor, as a recognition of worth, lies then at the very heart of God's own self, and its denial in sin is against the very core of God.

Sin as violation of God's law

John Calvin sees things differently. Instead of the honor of God being that against which sin is directed, for Calvin, generally speaking, that to which sin is contrary is God's law. Focusing in on what John Calvin has to say about sin and human nature is sort of like focusing on what Shakespeare said about love. It is such a wide-ranging and important notion, and simultaneously so subtly conceived, that it is hard to know where to begin. At the risk of gross oversimplification, however, the matter might be put like this. Authentic human existence is characterized by gratitude, which is the recognition that since God has secured my existence, I need not, and indeed cannot, secure it myself. Gratitude is the appropriate response, or correlate, to the anterior work of God's grace. Sin is exactly the obverse. Whether or not I am consciously ungrateful, when I sin I am turning away from God in an effort to secure my own existence, my own life's meaning, happiness, and justification. To do so is utter pride and presumptuousness, for only God is able to do this. Pride, understood as *autonomy*, or following the law of self, is therefore the antithesis of the anterior work of God.

Few theologians have placed the doctrines of God and humanity in such close proximity as has Calvin. His *Institutes* famously begins by saying "True and sound wisdom consists of only two parts: knowledge of God and knowledge of ourselves."[26] Those two ideas mutually condition and inform each other. Right knowledge of one both implies and creates right knowledge of the other. In the doctrine of creation, therefore, we would expect to learn as much about the Creator as we would the creature. Calvin's doctrine of creation comes early in the *Institutes*, and shows his essential continuity with much of the patristic and medieval tradition. God creates the universe as a theater of God's glory.[27] Humans are created last, and their being is found in appreciating the goodness of what God has made. In order to allow humans to do this, God has to give them some special gifts, like reason and intellect, but these gifts are intended only to serve the purpose of marveling at what God has done. This leads to Calvin's definition of the *imago Dei*, the image of God, which he describes as "the full possession of right understanding, when his affections were kept under sound reason, all his senses tempered in right order, and he truly referred his excellence to exceptional gifts bestowed upon him by his Maker."[28]

This definition is of extraordinary import in the history of theology. With the notable exception of Luther, Calvin's anthropology is among the first to be based less on a particular endowment or "faculty" than it is on a capacity for relationship. What it means to be a human is—of course in addition to reason and will and consciousness and so on—mostly to be in relationship with God and creation. And "sin" simply names the obverse of this in Calvin's theology. Adam's sin was not that he gave in to the temptation of Eve or the serpent, or that the sensuous flesh of the fruit represented a regression to Adam's baser and more physical qualities. Nor is it, for Calvin, a sin of pride that ushers in all the rest of the sins. This was what Calvin took Augustine's view to be.[29] Instead, original sin is unfaithfulness.[30] Excessive ambition, then pride, and finally ungratefulness issue from this original act of Adam casting aside faith and trust in his creator, and the following of one's own "law" rather than the law of God. The followers of Calvin who wrote some of the great Reformed confessions of faith were even clearer on this matter. Question 14 of the Westminster Shorter Catechism asks, "What is sin?" The answer is, "Sin is any want of conformity unto, or transgression of, the Law of God." The Heidelberg Catechism puts the matter like this:

Q.3: How do you come to know your misery?
A. The law of God tells me.
Q.4.What does God's law require of us?
A. Christ teaches us this in summary in Matthew 22—

Love the Lord your God with all your heart and with all your soul and with all your mind and with all your strength. This is the first and greatest commandment. And the second is like it: Love your neighbor as yourself.

All the Law and the Prophets hang on these two commandments.

The effect of original sin in the fallen human being is one of the celebrated themes of Calvin's theology and has been given the handy slogan of "total depravity." This has often been interpreted as the paragon of pessimistic anthropologies, leaving the human person to be merely a "five foot tall worm" (in Calvin's rhetoric).[31] Humans, on this view, are so repugnant that they are scarcely even redeemable. But this is overstatement. What Calvin's thoughts on sin seek to assert is that there is *no part of the human* that is left untouched by the effects of sin. All the "powers of the soul" are affected. Our ability to know God by our intellect is weakened. Our capacities in the sphere of "moral action" are severely compromised. But when Calvin writes that "original sin is the hereditary depravity and corruption of our nature, diffused into all parts of the soul," he means that there is no single part of the human being left unaffected by the powerful reality of sin.[32] Despite our sin, we are still able to muster a certain knowledge of God, at the very least in the *sensus divinitatis*.[33] We are able to achieve much in the way of secular learning—Calvin's thoughts on the achievements of humanism and the Renaissance are the subject of many volumes.[34] That is, there is no part of humanity that is completely obliterated, either. Total depravity means that in whichever sense the human is spoken of, fallenness must be included, but never considered to be exhaustive.

That Calvin conceived of sin as a rupture of God's law is quite clear. However, seeing Calvin's doctrine of creation and sin in the context of "gratitude and grace" is a viable, but not the only, way of organizing his theology.[35] Some scholars have tried to allow Calvin's biography to inform their readings of his theology, and so have suggested other means of problematizing and resolving human existence. Chief among these alternatives is ordering sin under the rubric of *anxiety*. Calvin's Geneva was a tiny, isolated enclave entirely surrounded by unsympathetic peoples. The success or failure of the Reformation was anything but a foregone conclusion, and the continued viability of the community of Geneva at all was uncertain. Couple that with Calvin's naturally anxious personality, and it is little wonder that his anthropology takes on that sense of anxiety. Calvin seems to have detested the liquidity of borders. Order was the paramount virtue. Sin as *disorder* was therefore the paramount vice. In fact, "mixture" was one of the worst things Calvin could say about something. Boundaries, on the other hand, were Calvin's favorite lines to draw.[36] The knowledge of where the boundaries are to be located comes exclusively from God's law, and sin is the refusal to abide by the map so established.[37]

Sin as denial of God's word

If honor is existentially close to one's deepest self, and law is the presence of the deepest self extended to others, then the notion that unites and crystallizes both is *word*. I *am* my word in a very deep way, but I also make myself present to others via my voice.[38] Many people remember the first time they heard their voice played back from a recording. In my case, as I listened to this strange person talking from the tape recorder, I recognized the words being said as those that I had uttered not long before. But that voice! Who was that strange-sounding ventriloquist co-opting me? The jarring dissonance of hearing your voice, and thus your words, as not your own, highlights the near identity of person and word.

So, for Martin Luther, sin is against God primarily in the sense that it is against his word.[39] God's word comprises two forms, the law and the gospel. Sin is the denial of either, or both, of the forms. Humans sin by refusing to believe that the law is the word of God and thus the rule of life, or that the gospel is both the truth about God and about humanity itself. The human heart is so deep that we cannot investigate it ourselves. We therefore need the word to show us the depth of sin.[40] We might know something about human sinfulness without the word, but the word is offered to help us to see that there is "little good in his nature and that whatever good there is, is misused."[41] The word of God looks at the human heart and finds there "unfaith at the bottom of the heart as the root and source of all sin."[42] Or again, "The main and real sin is unfaith, despising God, which is what takes place when a man does not fear, love and trust in God as he certainly should."[43] The effects of this unfaith are primarily manifested in the form of ingratitude, which highlights some of the continuities on this matter between Luther and Calvin.[44]

Sin for Luther is the replacement of God's word with one's own, the substitution of a God-directedness with a kind of self-centeredness. Not without good cause, Luther is well remembered for talking about sin as *cor incurvatus in se est*—the heart turned in on itself.[45] What makes matters "worse," according to Luther, is that our knowledge of this inwardly distorted orientation does nothing to help us amend it. We cannot do anything to repair the situation. God's word must continually come *extra nos*—from outside of ourselves—and continually kill and make alive again the sinner. Becoming properly exocentric is not a matter of effort, nor of knowledge.[46] As Luther scholar Paul Althaus puts it, "A man [sic] sins against God . . . even when he takes everything seriously, attempts to establish his own righteousness, and thereby shuts himself off from that righteousness which God wants to give. Man thus sins even when he does the best he can, even with his best works."[47] The sinful human, then, is unwilling (to say nothing of unable) to let the law of God rule his or her life, and is unable (to say nothing of unwilling) to believe the gospel truth that one's true center lies outside of oneself, that one's *telos* is blessedness in God's mercy, and that Christ has, in a "joyful exchange" actually taken one's sin onto himself and replaced them with his righteousness.[48] In denying the validity of the law and the truth of the gospel, the sinner negates the word of God.

*　*　*

In this brief tour through the thought worlds of Anselm, Calvin, and Luther we have seen that sin's good news consists in bringing God back into the picture of moral fault, and thus reintroducing the language of hope, forgiveness, and reconciliation into the experience of suffering and human misery. We have seen, however, that the way in which the "against-ness" of God is problematized is far from uniform. In fact, several other contraries could have been given. Thomas Aquinas, for example, speaks of sin as "any act or deed contrary to the eternal *will* of God."[49] The Catholic catechism speaks of sin as "an offense against reason, truth, and right conscience."[50] John Wesley tends to speak of sin as a willful rejection of the grace of God.[51] Throughout the pages of this book we will see many such diverging formulations, but each seeks to coordinate the reality of God with the facticity of human misery, and to do so in such a way that misery does not and cannot have the final word.

CHAPTER 2

APPROACHES TO SIN IN THE BIBLE

I know my transgressions, and my sin is always before me.
—*Psalm 51.3*

I'm looking for a loophole!
—*W.C. Fields, when asked why he, a confirmed atheist,
was reading the Bible on his death bed*

The person who expects to come to the Bible and find there a unified "theory" of sin will be disappointed. No such unity exists. What we find in the Bible with respect to sin is instead a kind of collage. Many different words in Hebrew (the language of the Old Testament or, as it is also known, the Hebrew Bible) and Greek (the language of the New Testament) are translated as "sin," and these words are as different from each other as they are similar. All imply something not being right in the complex relationships of oneself to God, oneself to one's neighbor, and oneself to oneself. Such views vary from a kind of mild "not living up to the possible" in such relationships to downright rebellion and open revolt. This chapter looks at the ways in which this range is thematized in the writings of the Bible.[1] Far from being simply a word study that looks at the discrete meanings of individual words for "sin," "evil," "iniquity," and so forth, this chapter seeks to approach the core meaning of sin's "against-ness." That is, I assume that many biblical writers have chosen to thematize the one phenomenon of sin—acts, intentions, dispositions, and states against God—in a variety of ways, but it really is one reality that is thereby so polyvalently described. In the following, then, though many descriptions of the human condition shall be presented, it is the one condition, and its one against-God-ness, that we seek to illuminate.

OLD TESTAMENT VOCABULARIES

Deviation

The Old Testament[2] does not tend to think of sin as a "thing" the way some other religious texts do. The language of sin as "stain" does not appear nearly as much in the OT as it does, for example, in the Upanishads.[3] Language for sin is not metaphysical, but metaphorical. At its most metaphorical, then, is the notion of sin as [ḥāṭā']. This is "to miss" or "to err." It is not a thing, but a moving away from. It is a missing, a falling short, a deviating. Such a notion requires not nouns, but gerunds. Consider the following nontheological OT examples of the meaning of [ḥāṭā']. Judges 20.16 reads, "Of all this force, there were seven hundred picked men who were left-handed; every one could sling a stone at a hair, *and not miss.*" And Proverbs 19.2 reads, "Desire without knowledge is not good, and one who moves too hurriedly *misses the way.*" In these examples, we see that [ḥāṭā'] can mean simply one physical object not traveling on the correct physical trajectory toward another physical object.

More usually, however, [ḥāṭā'] has a religious meaning, because the goal away from which one tends is either God himself or a creature for whom God's benevolent will desires care. For example, in Genesis 20.9 Abimelech accuses Abraham, saying, "How have I *sinned against you*, that you have brought such great guilt on me and my kingdom? You have done things to me that ought not to be done." Or again in Lamentations 5.7, we read, "Our ancestors *sinned*; they are no more, and we bear their iniquities." The implication in these texts is that a moral agent has acted without particular malice, and without conscious disregard for God's word, honor, or law, but that nonetheless in so acting has departed from the way that should be taken. Genesis 43.9 uses this same language, when Judah tells his father, "If I do not bring him back to you and set him before you, then let me *bear the sin* forever." Here we have the conscious desire to do what is right in the sight of God and God's creatures, but uncertainty about whether God's will can be done in this context. Views of this dimension of sin fill the pages of the OT. [ḥāṭā'] and various forms related to it appear some 300 times.[4] It occurs in every stratum of Hebrew history, from the most ancient texts to the Intertestamental literature and Apocrypha.[5] Psalm 58.3, for example, reads "The wicked go astray from the womb; they *err* from their birth, speaking lies." Ezekiel 44.10 carries a similar connotation when the prophet states, "But the Levites who went far from me, *going astray* from me after their idols when Israel went astray, shall bear their punishment." [ḥāṭā'] can sometimes have the concrete connotation of an erring away from God's direct command, as in Numbers 14.41, where Moses says, "Why do you continue to *transgress the command* of the Lord? That will not succeed." Sometimes there is also a cultic significance connected to [ḥāṭā'], in the sense that because of this erring a kind of expiatory sacrifice or prayer needs to be performed in the temple by a priest. Such instances are the exception rather than the rule, however. Generally speaking, there is a kind of nebulous, metaphorical straying, or departing, from the way that we should go connoted by [ḥāṭā'].

Rebellion

Sin is not just something that happens because we aim for the right goal, try to go down the right path, or have the right intentions, but simply miss the mark. There is also in sin a kind of active seeking of the wrong goals or paths, and having the wrong intentions. Sin is not just deviation, it is also active rebellion. This is denoted in the OT by the word [pesha']. This word is used less frequently in the OT, and its use is reserved for a very intense description and denunciation of sin. [pesha'] implies a conscious, willful disobedience. As with [ḥāṭā'], which has theological and nontheological meanings, [pesha'] can sometimes imply simply earthly rebellion against a ruler. For example, 1 Kings 12.19 reads, "So Israel has been in *rebellion* against the house of David to this day." Or 2 Kings 1.1 states, "After the death of Ahab, Moab *rebelled* against Israel." These political, nonreligious valences of [pesha'] carry over into the theological view of sin as rebellion. Job 33.9 reads, "You say, 'I am clean, without rebellion; I am pure, and there is no iniquity in me.'"

The object of the against-ness of rebellion is not always constant. Very often the implication is that the sinner revolts by breaking a commandment, or law (e.g. Jeremiah 3.13, Hosea 8.1). But sometimes the against-ness is directed toward God as such, not an extension of God, like God's honor, word, or law (e.g. Isaiah 1.2, Hosea 7.13). In addition to [pesha'], several other words also imagine sin to be revolt or rebellion. The slightly less intense word [mārad] means "to act disrespectfully" and in consequence "to rebel," and is found in, for example, Ezek. 2.3, Num. 14.9, and Josh. 22.19. [Mārā] means "to contend against" and can be found, for example, in Num. 20.24,

Ps. 105.28, and Lam. 3.42. Finally, [sārar or sur] means "to be stubbornly rebellious" and is frequently used to describe those who not only consciously begin to rebel against God or his commandment, but also persist willfully in doing so (e.g. Isaiah 30.1, Hosea 9.15, Jeremiah 6.28).

Burden of guilt

In addition to intentional or unintentional deviation from a path and active rebellion against God, a third significant way the OT thematizes sin is with the term ['wn]. This term, often translated "iniquity" is really the comingling of sin and the guilt that it causes. Guilt is understood here both as culpability and as a feeling of guilt, or the burden that being guilty places on oneself. Genesis 4.13, for example, quotes Cain regretting both his iniquity against God by killing Abel, and the punishment that he thereby incurred. Or again, Daniel 9.13 reads, "Just as it is written in the law of Moses, all this calamity has come upon us. We did not entreat the favor of the Lord our God, turning from our *iniquities* and reflecting on his fidelity."

Very frequently the implication is that ['wn] is like a heavy weight, or a burden. A common phrase that is translated "to forgive a sin" (nasa' 'wn) most literally means "to remove a burden."[6] We see this in such places as Genesis 50.17 and Exodus 10.17, in which sins are forgiven by those humans who have been wronged. But bearing the burden of sin is something that also belongs to the very nature of God. The well-known passage from Num 14.18 reads, "The Lord is slow to anger, and abounding in steadfast love, *forgiving iniquity and transgression.*" The last phrase there literally means "bearing away the burden of sin." Sin is a weight that becomes, collectively speaking, so heavy that only God can carry the burden, and so final forgiveness necessarily must come from God, not from his creatures.

Numerous other words are used in the OT to describe and denounce sin and its effects. Humans can "cross over" ['ābar] a boundary, in the sense of transgressing the limits set by God's law. Persons who habitually do so are "profane" [hānep̄] or "wicked" [bēliyyaal]. Occasionally, individual sins are highlighted as being "taboo" [tō'ēbā, shiqqûts] in the sense that they are utterly contrary to God's intentions and thus are abominations.[7] There is also a range of words referring to cultic offenses, meaning those actions related to the temple and its worship [šggh/šggt].[8] The prophets consistently denounce other bad human actions, such as particular crimes against the public order, dishonesty, and oppression of the weak. Given this extraordinarily broad and deep variety of ways that humanity's "against-God-ness" is used in the OT, we must come to the conclusion that sin and its related concepts are of the utmost importance to the writers of the OT, and ought to be, too, for those who claim to follow the message it proclaims.

SIN IN TORAH

The first five books of the Old Testament are known as the Pentateuch, or Torah. Torah is a rich Hebrew word meaning, fundamentally, "law" or, perhaps better, "instruction." Unlike the English word "law" that has, for some, fairly negative connotations, Torah is unambiguously positive. Anyone who has traveled to a country where justice is administered by personal bribe or by threat of physical violence knows what a relief it is to have the rule of law. Laws, when just, actually promote freedom, rather than repress it. I experience the freedom of, say, a long road trip most effectively when I and others follow the rules of the road. I am freest in a society in which I cede some of my potential freedoms in order to gain other kinds of freedom. So sin in Torah is that which binds freedom or frustrates its ends.

Beginning at the beginning, we see a kind of trajectory of sin evident in the first several chapters of Genesis. According to the stories we find there, God creates the world to be good—this point is repeated many times—and on the sixth day, God surveys all that has been made and declares it to be "very good."[9] Part of the thrust of this way of telling the creation story is to affirm that God does not directly cause sin. God has neither erroneously nor maliciously brought about a creation that is 90 percent good and 10 percent fallen. But quickly the goodness of creation comes undone, and its demise is a kind of unfolding pattern of transgression. Imagine a pebble thrown into a pool of water. Ripples emanate from the center. This is true of sin in Genesis 3–11.

The first ripple is sin at the level of the individual. Eve succumbs to the temptation of the serpent and eats of the fruit of the tree of the knowledge of good and evil, and Adam does the same. Here we have a problem with the will of the individual; it does not know that it is not good for the creature to want something that contradicts God's commandment. Or if it does know this fact, it does not care.

Whereas sin in Greek philosophy, and in the thought patterns of many of Israel's neighbors, is fundamentally connected with ignorance—if a moral agent truly knew enough about possible actions, the good would always be chosen—sometimes the moral agent simply has a distorted, wicked will that chooses contrary to the good.

The second ripple is a break in the family. After Adam and Eve are expelled from the Garden, the next major story line is the tragedy between their sons, the brothers Cain and Abel. Angry that Abel's sacrifice is looked upon favorably by God, and that his own is not, Cain lures his brother into a field and kills him. No longer is the individual alone affected by sin; now the family unit has become involved. Cain has to travel to a place called Nod (a wordplay on the Hebrew word for "wander") and then meets his wife and begins another family, worried about the consequences of his sin and the vengeance he fears may come. First the individual will is distorted in sin, and now, one emanation farther out, the integrity of families has become compromised.[10]

A collection of individuals is a family, and a collection of families is a community. In the next major story line of Genesis, we see the third ripple of sin—the community at large has become corrupted. At the heart of the story of the sin of community is wickedness that has worked its way into all aspects of society. Genesis 6.5–6 reads, "The Lord saw that the wickedness of humankind was great in the earth, and that every inclination of the thoughts of their hearts was only evil continually. And the Lord was sorry that he had made humankind on the earth, and it grieved him to his heart." The particular sins of the people are never enumerated. The law had not yet been given to Moses, so conscious transgression of the law was not understood to be behind the sin of mankind. God's covenant had not yet been made with Noah, and an "Adamic covenant" was not part of Israel's self-understanding until well after the verses listed above were written.[11] The evil done by humankind remains vague in content, but specific in gravity: the goodness of creation is ripped apart by sin.

Sin spreads so far as its effects ripple outward from Eden that some have even thought that the divinity itself may have been affected by the fall. This is, of course, a controversial, and by no means widely held, view. But a curious passage in Gen. 6.1–4 captures our attention. There we read about the "Nephilim," identified as "sons of God" of giant stature. They are not quite God, not really human.

They could be, and have been, thought of as god-like, quasi-divine creatures. They lusted after human women and sired children by them. The fact that God's destruction of the Earth begins in the very next verse implies divine fury over this situation.[12] Whether or not the tide of sin swells all the way into the divine itself, the trajectory of sin in Torah leaves the unmistakable impression of a very good world gone very wrong.[13]

One brief note on the notion of the goodness of creation in Genesis will complete our look at sin in Torah. God creates in two ways, according to Genesis. First, God creates *ex nihilo*, that is, "out of nothing."[14] God makes what is out of what wasn't. Second, and for our purposes, more importantly, God creates by separating. God takes some of the water of the "waste and void" (Gen. 1.1) and puts it on the one side and puts the rest on the other. In the middle, dry land is created. God takes all of the light and puts it on the one side, and it's day. The other side is night. Once creatures are made, part of the integrity of creation comes from the fish *not* being the bird; the man is *not* the woman. Thus the goodness of creation comes from the honoring of these distinctions. Conversely, sin and evil enter creation when these distinctions are not honored. The serpent tells Eve that if she eats of the fruit of the tree of the knowledge of good and evil, she will be *like God* (Gen. 3.5). But part of the created goodness of Eve is that she is Eve, *not* God. So in eating the fruit, she crosses the limit that is, in fact, life-giving. Some of the language of wickedness in the flood story calls to mind sexual impropriety and general violence. Such actions may be understandable for other creatures in the animal kingdom, but not for humans. By not honoring the distinction between human nature and animal nature, humans sin. So too, in our discussion of the Nephilim, we saw that it is good for there to be an untransgressed boundary between the divine and the human natures. Sin happens when such distinctions are not honored. In fact, the whole of Torah makes this one point in continually unfolding ways.

SIN IN THE PROPHETS

The largest corpus of writings in the OT comprises the books of the prophets. The essential message of a prophet in ancient Israel and in Israel's sacred writings was twofold: prophets might "foretell" or "forthtell." Foretelling is the prediction of a future yet to come, or a holding up of a vision of a future toward which one might work or away from which one might try to veer. Forthtelling, on the other hand, involves the denunciation of a present state of affairs either on the basis of just such a vision or on the basis of a creative construal of the past. For instance, the books of the "former prophets," Joshua, Judges, 1 and 2 Samuel, and 1 and 2 Kings, are not really predictions of the future at all, but rather histories of the development of Israel from the resettlement of the land of Palestine after the exodus from Egypt through the first centuries of Israel's kings.

This prompts an interesting question. If history is about the past, and prophecy is about the future, how can *history* be prophetic? The answer is, when the sins of Israel's past are told in a compelling way that speaks to the present time, a repetition of that history can be avoided. Some nonbiblical examples of this phenomenon may help to clarify things. Arthur Miller's play *The Crucible* is not only an account of the seventeenth century witch trials in Salem, it is also an indictment of McCarthyism in 1950s America. The film and, later, television show *M*A*S*H* is not only a series of stories about medical personnel during the Korean war, it is also an indictment of the Vietnam war, which was underway when the film and much of the series first aired. So too, the books of the former prophets are not only histories of kingships and problems in Israel's past. They also forthtell—in the sense of bringing forth judgment—on the "present" situation of the prophet's own first audience, and maybe even on our own present.

Consequently, what we see in the prophetic literature is not at all a generalized theory of human nature (though the prophets do occasionally reflect on such issues) and its disruption in sin, but rather a specification of particular actions and dispositions likely to bring God's wrath or blessing. The refrain of the author of much of the former prophets is "Israel did what was evil in the sight of the Lord." Over and over and over again, this phrase appears in the writings of the Deuteronomist, who wrote Joshua, Judges, 1 and 2 Samuel, and 1 and 2 Kings, in addition to Deuteronomy.[15] And almost always, the "evil" that is done is the worship of foreign Gods. It was not just the actual apostasy of bowing down to the Canaanite gods that is singled out for censure in the former prophets. Rather, what the Deuteronomist seeks to denounce is the lack of total devotion to the one God of Israel that would allow, in principle, such idol worship. Deut. 6.4 offers a kind of synopsis of the whole series of the seven books from the Deuteronomic perspective. It reads, "Hear, O Israel: The Lord is our God, the Lord alone." The God of Israel is alone sovereign. As such, he requires not the *partial* allegiance due to any one of a number of gods in a polytheistic pantheon. Rather, the God of Israel demands and deserves *total* allegiance and love. Any action that does not spring from this generative pulse is, at its root, sin.[16]

When we move to the books of the latter prophets we see a kind of a shift. Whereas the former prophets speak mostly of the general life orientation that does not embrace strict monotheism as the root sin, the latter prophets speak of the concrete sinful acts committed by the "heart" that has been corrupted. Thus Isaiah quotes God as saying "these people draw near with their mouths and honor me with their lips, while their hearts are far from me." (Isa. 29.13) Similarly, Jeremiah 17.9 reads, "The heart is deceitful above all else; it is perverse. Who can understand it?" The heart is understood as the basis for the will, not the emotions or intellect. A corrupt heart, therefore, will eventuate in wicked, sinful actions. In Jeremiah's words, "But they say, 'It is no use! We will follow our own plans, and each of us will act according to the stubbornness of our evil heart'" (Jer. 18.12) and, "But they did not listen or pay attention; instead, they followed the stubbornness of their evil hearts" (Jer. 11.8).

Rather than psychologizing into the nature or the cause of the sinful "heart," the latter prophets tend to identify and critique the sinful acts such a heart produces. When Isaiah is called to be a prophet in the Jerusalem temple, he protests by saying, "Woe is me! I am lost, for I am a man of unclean lips, and I live among a people of unclean lips; . . . Then one of the seraphs flew to me, holding a live coal that had been taken from the altar with a pair of tongs. The seraph touched my mouth with it and said: 'Now that this has touched your lips, your guilt has departed and your sin is blotted out'" (Isa. 6.5–7). Isaiah then lists wicked acts of his countrymen and -women that constitute such "uncleanness."

These acts include, but are by no means limited to, rebellion, dishonesty, violence, theft, covenant disloyalty, inappropriate worship, and blasphemy. As the prophets understood it, sin involved an opposition of wills and allegiances. The will of the Creator and the will of the creature are at odds. For the latter prophets, as Walther Eichrodt summarizes, "Sin was comprehended as a conscious and responsible act, by which Man [sic] rebelled against the unconditional authority of God in order to decide for himself what way he should take, and to make God's gifts serve his own ego."[17] The one who is so self-serving cannot see anything else. The whole world is transformed from being an array of beloved creatures of God whose needs should be cared for into being a supply of potentially manipulable instruments that can be crafted to serve the ends of the sinful heart. The most common way of criticizing this self-centeredness is in the disregard shown by Israel for the widow, the orphan, and the otherwise powerless. In short, the prophets show the symptoms of sin as especially present when the poor are mistreated.

One place to see the significance placed on the sin of mistreatment of the poor is in the text of Amos. Amos was a prophet who was active in the eighth century BC, when the Northern Kingdom of Israel and the Southern Kingdom of Judah were keeping a watchful eye on the military advances of their dreaded enemy to the northeast, Assyria. The Assyrians were well known for terrorizing those they conquered with particularly brutal violence. Amos prophesied mostly in the region of Bethel, in the Northern Kingdom, and his message speaks to the impending doom of an Assyrian invasion. To understand Amos' particular perspective on sin, a brief bit of background must be shared.

The reigns of King Uzziah (783–742 BC) in the north and King Jeroboam II (786–746 BC) in the south were very prosperous years in both lands. Trade routes that had been closed for years were reopened. The political stability inherent in such long reigns of kings usually portended economic stability, as well. Evidence shows that commerce between Israel, Judah, and the Transjordan opened up in previously unseen ways. By all accounts, the economy was booming.

And yet, Amos warns that those who have benefitted from such economic success are bringing God's judgment on the nation, for they have used their wealth unjustly. The book of Amos begins with a series of oracles against several nations, declaring their disfavor in the sight of God, and enumerating the main sins that justify their harsh judgment. The list begins with Damascus and winds its way through a variety of rivals of Israel and Judah. Consider Table 2.1, which outlines the kingdom against which an oracle is spoken, the sins committed that Amos singles out for special denunciation, and the prediction of God's justice visited upon that nation.

One could imagine Amos standing on the steps of the temple at Bethel giving a speech consisting of these oracles.[18] Bystanders would be attracted to the thought of their old enemies around them being judged by God for their wickedness. As Amos goes down the list,

Table 2.1 Oracles of judgment in Amos

Kingdom	Major sin	Judgment
Damascus	Treating Gilead harshly in defeat	City gate broken, people exiled
Gaza	Selling captives into slavery	Fire sent on city, remnant dies
Tyre	Selling slaves, forgetting covenants	Fire sent on city's forts
Edom	Using war captives as slaves in mines	Fire sent on city
Ammonites	Horribly cruel war practices	King exiled, city burned
Moab	Disrespecting royal remains	King killed, city burned
Judah	Not following God's law	Fire sent, strongholds burned
Israel	Mistreatment of poor	Israel "pressed down into place" by God

their applause might grow louder and louder as the judgment is proclaimed. But then, when Amos denounces Judah, the crowd would be hushed. Though the kingdoms of the north and south had separated, still they were one people, coreligionists and sons and daughters of Abraham, Isaac, and Jacob. When their lawlessness is condemned, Amos would have their full attention. And when his fiery message turned directly to the people whom he was addressing, we can easily imagine the shocked faces of those around him.

Here is what our imagined crowd would have heard was the sin of Israel so terrible that God's judgment would be brought upon them:

> Thus says the Lord: For three transgressions of Israel, and for four, I will not revoke the punishment; because they sell the righteous for silver, and the needy for a pair of sandals—they who trample the head of the poor into the dust of the earth, and push the afflicted out of the way; father and son go in to the same girl, so that my holy name is profaned; they lay themselves down beside every altar on garments taken in pledge; and in the house of their God they drink wine bought with fines they imposed.[19]

Let two final points be made in our discussion of "social sin" in Amos. The nation that would be most expected to be worthy of God's punishment, to the ears of Amos' audience, would have been Assyria. Yet the Assyrians are never named. And secondly, in their stead, Israel is not only named, but nearly equated with their hated enemy

Assyria. One thing that the Assyrian army was known for was their practice of trampling the corpses of soldiers whose armies they had defeated.[20] After the bodies had been lying in the sun decomposing for a time, the Assyrians made a ritual of stomping on the bodies, such that in their distended, bloated state they might even rupture. Thus when Amos alleges that the people of Israel "trample the head of the poor into the dust of the earth" he is perhaps deliberately calling to mind the particular atrocities of the Assyrians.

A WISDOM MISCELLANY

Much of the OT speaks of God in highly specified terms, noting his particular acts in the history of a particular people, Israel. But not all literature in the OT follows this pattern. Wisdom literature refers to books like Proverbs, Job, Ecclesiastes, some of the Psalms (e.g. Ps. 37), and, in the Apocrypha, The Wisdom of Solomon and Ecclesiasticus. The focus in Wisdom literature is not specifically on the exact nature of the God said to be revealed in the great saving acts of Israel's history, but rather what can be known about the divine, and about the creation, by all people. The purpose of the wise Hebrew sage was to communicate the truths derived from hard-won lessons of experience. The opposite of a good life is not a sinful one, necessarily, but rather one characterized by foolishness, by folly. Thus we see less of an emphasis placed on sin *per se*. Proverbs 8.36 speaks of sin in the sense of someone who "fails" to find wisdom or "misses" it when it could be seen. The presumption remains that wicked actions are, in some sense, against God (e.g. Prov. 3.32–34), but this is understood in such a way as to have practical, not apocalyptic, consequences (Prov. 1.24–33). Those who, in general, followed the dictates of wisdom would, in general, be blessed, while those who obstinately refused to welcome wisdom would speak of having incurred God's wrath.

The book of Proverbs lists a series of "abominations" that the wise know are hated by God. The list includes, primarily, offenses against other persons. Singled out for special censure are: dishonesty, trickery, conspiracy or scheming against another person, instigating argument, and wrongly punishing the innocent. These are "sins" only in the derivative sense of being contrary to what God wills for other creatures, and strictly theological language is almost never used here or elsewhere regarding sin in the Wisdom literature.[21] When the preacher of the book of Ecclesiastes notes, in 7.20, "Surely there is no one on earth so righteous as to do good without ever sinning," he does so in a universalistic context. He is remarking on the uniformity of human experiences across time and space—all have acted wrongly from time to time, even when seeking out what is good.[22]

NEW TESTAMENT VOCABULARIES

Since much of the conceptual framework, and even direct wording, for the New Testament[23] comes from the Greek version of the OT, called the Septuagint, we might expect that some of the vocabulary for sin would be borrowed from the diverse ways sin was thematized in the Old Testament. And examination of the NT writings bears this out. Many of the NT words for sin and its related concepts are directly borrowed from the Septuagint. We consider here hamartia, meaning primarily discrete acts of deviation, sin as a total way of being, sin as debt, and sin as absence of righteousness.

Deviation

Just as one of the most common ways of talking about sin in the OT was [ḥāṭā'], which in its nontheological valence means "erring" or "straying from the path," by far the most common NT word for sin is the Septuagint translation of that word, *hamartia*. This word has a long history in Greek thought. Homer's *Illiad*, for example, uses the word more than 100 times to describe a spear that is thrown but does not hit its mark. The Greek historian Thucydides frequently uses the term to describe a traveler who loses his way. However, in the NT the word has only its ethical and theological meanings, in the sense that the one who has acted in this way, or has become a *hamartalos*, a sinner, has missed the moral and religious mark, or lost the way of righteousness. The extent of the deviation varies. All NT authors would agree that sin is universal in the sense that everyone "occasionally sins." Yet some would say that there are heavier and lighter sins, such as Hebrews 10 and 1 John 3. And there is a sense in which the deviation is total. Jesus came to call, and to befriend, "tax collectors and sinners" (Mt. 11.19, Lk. 7.34), whose entire lives are contradictory to the intentions of God. A variety of words in addition to *hamartia* are used, such as *parabasis* (transgression), *parapton* (falling aside), and *parakon* (to turn one's ear away from). All have the sense of turning away from the proper orientation or path.

Sinners

The noun "sinner" in the NT means either, (1) one who habitually breaks the customs and laws of Torah, (2) one who understands that sin has affected and infected all people, and (3) the ordinary folk, the *hoi polloi*, who were not educated enough to understand the finer points of the law, or who could not as a rule be expected to live up to the highest ethical and religious standards. For an example of sense (1), we could turn to Luke 7.36–50. In this passage, Jesus is dining with a group of Pharisees. As they are about to begin their meal, a woman enters the room, bends down to Jesus's feet, and washes them with her tears and dries them with her hair. We know virtually nothing about this woman, except that Luke identifies her as "a sinner."[24] The implication of the story is that all present at the meal know that she is a sinner. This might not mean that she is a fundamentally totally wicked person. Some in Galilee and Judea simply did not always fulfill the law as a matter of habit. Some were forced to work on the Sabbath, for example, or had jobs that frequently caused them not to maintain the strictest purity.[25]

Some have argued along the lines of sense (3) above, that *hamartalos* refers to the lowly dregs of society—the "*am ha'arets*," or "people of the land." Following the law was complicated, and the Pharisees asserted that in order to obey the law, every jot and tittle of both the Written Torah and Oral Torah had to be followed. This required both a certain amount of time—for example, time to cook according to the dietary laws—as well as a certain amount of money.[26]

Debt

Jesus's famous prayer in Matthew's version asks God to "forgive us our debts, as we forgive our debtors" (Mt. 6.12). The economic metaphor for sin as a debt incurred both to God and to neighbor is used twice. Luke's version of the prayer reads, "forgive us our sins, for we ourselves forgive everyone indebted to us" (Lk. 11.4). There one usage of the monetary term is omitted, but it is still used once. The Greek term used here is ὀφειλέτης. We see the notion of sin as a "debt" to be repaid elsewhere, such as Lk. 13.4, in which the victims of the falling tower at Siloam are not thought to be greater "sinners" (ὀφειλέτης) than any others, and in Rom. 8.12 it seems to be used as a general word for all those who are burdened with life "in the flesh."

It is also used less with a religious connotation than an ethical one in Rom. 1.14, 15.27, and Gal. 5.3.

Absence of righteousness

In Greek, the prefix "a" denotes a privative, or a lack. For example, one who believes in God is a theist, and one who does not is an atheist. One who sins, by this same logic, is one who does not possess righteousness, or piety, or godliness. The main words used to represent sin in this way are ἀδικία (unrighteousness or injustice) and ἀσέβεια (impiety). ἀδικία often, though not always, refers to sin's horizontal cast, in the sense that one acts unjustly against other people (e.g. Lk. 13.17), and ἀσέβεια to sin's vertical cast, in the sense that one acts in conscious, flagrant disregard for God's honor and law (e.g. Jude 15, 18; 2 Tim. 2.16). Since these notions of sin are entirely parasitic on the notions of the good they presuppose, further discussion of the words themselves will not lead us very far.

SIN IN THE GOSPELS

Each of the four canonical gospels, as well as Acts, seems to assume that sin is a universal phenomenon. In the opening scene of Mark, John the Baptist appears in the wilderness, "proclaiming a baptism of repentance for the forgiveness of sins," and Jesus speaks of this same need of forgiveness (Mark 1.4, 15). Matthew quotes an angel of the Lord who says, "She will bear a son, and you are to name him Jesus, for he will save his people from their sins" (Matthew 1.21). Luke 1.77, John 1.29, and Acts 2.28 all share this same basic content. Never are certain people singled out as the ones who are especially responsible, nor the specific misdeeds named. The implication seems to be that sin has infected all people, at all times, everywhere, and forgiveness will be both required and possible.

The gospels do imply that Jesus associates with a particular subset of his culture that was *particularly* sinful, however (e.g. Mt. 11.19, Mk. 2.16). He was criticized, we are told, for advocating the repentance of those sinners and their subsequent acceptability before God. Surely the Pharisees whom Jesus knew, or those people who had been wronged by corrupt tax collectors or brutal tyrants, would not object to their debts being repaid or an attempt at reparations being made. So why would Jesus's message of repentance and forgiveness for "sinners" be so controversial? The answer must be that Jesus did not require, in addition to such actions as mentioned above, any further participation in the ritual, sacrificial atoning system of his day (e.g. commissioning a sacrifice at the temple). Rather, the grace that was present in Jesus himself was sufficient for forgiveness and welcome into the embrace of God, far apart from any sacrificial efficacy (cf. Heb. 10.1–18). Jesus was criticized both for associating with and for forgiving such people, and also for *being* such a person (Jn. 9.16, 24–25, 31). That Jesus Christ would be a sinner is contrary to much traditional Christian thinking and must, in some sense, be false. But that he was accused of identifying so closely with sinners that he would be called one is a strong claim. Though he does so in a much different way, Paul, too, claims that Jesus Christ became the "curse" of sin (Gal. 3.13) or that God "made him to be sin who knew no sin (2 Cor. 5.21). To the Apostle Paul we now turn.

PAUL ON SIN

Paul's views on sin have drawn sustained reflection and generated considerable scholarly dispute. Virtually no one disputes, however, that the notion of sin is certainly central to his theology. Paul views sin in at least two different ways. First, for Paul, one's whole life is to be oriented to the gospel and person of Jesus Christ. To the extent that it is not, it is sinful. Thus sin is any kind of orientation that is not Christ-centered. Paul writes in Rom. 14.23, "Whatever does not proceed from faith is sin." Concretely, this often takes the shape of elevating something that is not the gospel, something that does not "bear Christ," to use the terminology of Luther, up to divine status. This, in other words, is idolatry. When one thinks that such reliance on the idol will bring to the idolater the blessings and benefits of salvation, then the idolater is likely to speak about the benefits he has received. This is the underlying conceptuality of one of Paul's preferred metaphors for sin: boasting [καύχησις]. The righteousness of God the creator is so magnificent as to require the surrender of all human claims and "pretensions." Here is the logic behind one important Pauline passage on sin, Rom. 1.18–32. There God "gives up" sinners to the dishonoring of their creaturely goodness, through which they pretentiously seek to be wise, but end up fools (Rom. 1.22). Their so-called "knowledge" becomes a lie, and in their ignorance they serve the creature rather than the splendid creator (Rom. 1.25). This leads to a life characterized by a "debased mind," which makes decisions about acting in a way that always produces "things that should not be done" (Rom. 1.28).

The other dimension that Paul sees in sin is that sin is not just a characteristic of certain acts performed by sinful people. In fact, sin is a power, or a force, that is itself actively pernicious. When Paul discusses sin as a power, it is as if the universe has come to life in God-thwarting ways. Sin literally has a life of its own. It is not even the sinner who commits the sin, in one way of Paul's thinking, but rather the power of sin itself which is active, and the human being which is passive. The human being is not the subject of sinful acts, but their object. Sin, as a power of the "present evil age" (Gal. 1.4), rebels against the just power of God. Yet Paul does not think of sin as a disembodied power acting on its own. To put it another way, *sin* always acts in and through *sinners*. Where there is one, there is the other.

The notion of sin as power is closely linked to Paul's notion of "the flesh." We must immediately forestall a misunderstanding: Paul's linkage of sin and flesh is NOT a denunciation of all things bodily, or sexual, nor is it to reduce sin to sensuousness and lust. Rather, Paul thinks that the flesh is a slave to the law of sin (Rom. 7.25). One who gives oneself to the "passions and desires" of the flesh (Rom. 13.14, Gal. 5.24) reaches for a lower goal, obeys a lower law, leads a lower life, than one should. Paul contrasts the life that is lived "according to the flesh" (Rom. 8.4–5, 12–13) with the life that is lived "according to the spirit" (again, Rom. 8.4–5, 12–13). The flesh itself, by which Paul means humankind's creatureliness and the perceived exigencies that go with mortality, can so thoroughly co-opt one's attention that one's true life in God is ignored. The flesh in itself is not bad; on this point Paul differentiates his position from that of the Gnostics, Platonists, and others.[27] Paul can conceive of life dwelling "in the flesh" in ways not at all contrary to God's intentions (e.g. 2 Cor. 10.3, Rom. 2.28) or sinful. But fleshliness leads to sin and is exploited by sin's power when the human being becomes so concerned with the demands of the flesh that he is unconcerned with the demands of God and becomes incapable of serving God (Rom. 8.8–10). In privileging the demands of the flesh (or of the law, the determinant of the flesh), the human turns to oneself instead of seeing life as a gift from God (1 Cor. 4.7).

More needs to be said about the nexus of sin, flesh, and the third player in the Paul's logic of sin as power, namely, the law. Usually when Paul uses the word "law" [Gk. νομός] he means the Torah, or the law of Moses. He asserts in very strong terms that the law is not simply the same thing as sin, only under another name (Rom. 7.7). Sin was present in the world even before the law was given (e.g. Rom. 5.13), so an easy equivalence cannot be drawn. The law might "multiply sin" (Rom. 7.8) and produce "knowledge of sin" (Rom. 3.20), but even when the law is fulfilled, sin can use the law as its agent. When one obeys successfully all that the law requires,[28] one might be duped into thinking that one had thereby secured "the promise of life" (Rom. 7.10). But in thinking this, one would be completely mistaken. To summarize, then, the law is the agent of sin, and the flesh is the host of sin.[29]

Paul's language of sin as an enslaving power is not unique among the vocabularies and thought patterns of the New Testament. For example, Hebrews 3.13 warns Christians not to be "hardened by the deceitfulness of sin." But Paul is unique in the array of verbs he gives sin "to do." In Paul's way of thinking, sin is active enough to "have dominion" (at least hypothetically, in Rom. 6.14) and "reign" (Rom. 6.12) in one's body, it "seizes opportunities" (Rom. 7.8), "revives" itself (Rom. 7.10), and even "works death through what is good" (Rom. 7.13). Paul takes sin as a power alien to God with such seriousness that he even thinks it sometimes wins the cosmic struggle against him (Rom. 7.4–6). Since Paul accords so much agency to sin in "the present age," he actually makes relatively little of the notion of repentance, which is in contrast so critical in the gospels.[30]

It is instructive to note that, though Paul certainly describes, contextualizes, and elucidates sin, he does not ever seek to explain it or its origins. Even if Paul has a carefully conceived doctrine of original sin (a view which has been the subject of significant debate in recent decades),[31] he does not give an explanation for the fall itself. In Rom. 3.28 and Rom. 5.13, Paul states that sin and its consequences and guilt extend to all people, not just those to whom the law of Moses was given, and thus was, in principle, knowingly "transgressable." The origins of sin, in Paul's thought, can only be known by surmises based on what Paul does say. Two possibilities exist. First, Paul may have absorbed elements of a kind of dualistic worldview from his philosophical contemporaries. This would explain references in Paul to "so-called gods" (1 Cor. 8.5), "beings that by nature are not gods" (Gal. 4.8), "demons" (1 Cor. 10.20), or the "god of this age" (2 Cor 4.4 and 1 Cor. 2.6). We see a kind of metaphysical and moral dualism in the Essene writings of Paul's contemporaries at the Dead Sea. It is not unlikely that Paul could have employed such terminology and thought structures in his own—admittedly nondualistic—theology. The other possibility is that Paul simply deduced the universality of sin from its opposite; since he was convinced of the universality of God's grace extending to all people through the cross of Jesus Christ, then logically all people must be in need of such grace, and all people must somehow be guilty. Both possible solutions to the problem of the origins of sin in Paul's thought seem plausible, and do not necessarily exclude each other.

Perhaps the best way to read Paul on the nature and effects of sin is not to assume that he has a full-fledged theological anthropology already worked out, which then perfectly anticipates the solution to the plight of humankind. While there is prevenient grace, there need not be "prevenient sin"! On the contrary, the central feature, the beating heart, of Paul's theology and ethics is the message of the blessedness available to all who are connected to the grace of Jesus Christ in faith. The insights Paul has into sin come from his understanding of grace, not vice versa. Sin is known first, and best, in its defeat.

CHAPTER 3

ORIGINAL SIN AND THE LEGACY OF AUGUSTINE

Christianity preaches an obviously unattractive idea, such as original sin; but when we wait for its results, they are pathos and brotherhood and a thunder of laughter and pity; for only with original sin can we at once pity the beggar and distrust the king.
— *G.K. Chesterton, Orthodoxy*

The doctrine of original sin is the only empirically verifiable doctrine of the Christian faith.
— *Reinhold Niebuhr, quoting London Times Literary Supplement, in Man's Nature and His Communities*

Western theology is a series of footnotes to St. Augustine.
— *Jaroslav Pelikan, The Chrisitan Tradition: A History of the Development of Doctrine*

In his fascinating book exploring the nature and taxonomy of accounts of evil, Paul Ricoeur makes the following left-handed defense of the Christian notion of original sin. "Man [sic] is not the origin of evil; *man finds evil and continues it . . .* Evil is as old as the oldest of beings."[1] The insight contained therein is one that can be experientially corroborated by virtually any reflective person. To begin evil from scratch is virtually never our experience. Others have acted wrongly, creating difficult situations in which we find ourselves and in which we act wrongly ourselves. Evil is *continued*, not inaugurated, by each new human moral agent. Though there is more to original sin than just this one insight, nonetheless it speaks compellingly to an experience many can affirm. Though it has had several different expressions, and all manner of detractors and critics, the Christian notion of original sin remains a powerful and helpful series of proposals regarding the human condition. This chapter seeks to elucidate a few key characteristics of the doctrine of original sin, paying especially close attention to the one figure most closely associated with it, St. Augustine. Our story does not begin with him, however, since Augustine inherited a rich tradition of reflection on the origin of sin and human nature from a variety of sources. To them we now turn.

DEVELOPMENTS BEFORE AUGUSTINE

In the first few centuries of Christianity, the language of theological reflection was primarily Greek. The New Testament had been written in Greek, and the gospel had not taken root in the western part of the Mediterranean world (where Latin was the more common language) as quickly as it did in the eastern part. So the thought patterns, as well as the actual language, of theology, followed those of the Hellenistic world. When we look at understandings of sin, consequently, we see that the earliest Christian thinkers had a view of human nature and its corruption that was not altogether different from the philosophers around them. The human was held in high regard, capable of much good and endowed of a particular rational power. The rival philosophy of the time to the various forms of Hellenistic thought was Manichaeism. This school of thought taught that the material world and everything associated with it—desires, bodies, foods, other physical things—were evil and to be avoided by any means necessary. If one views Manichaeism as an unsavory alternative, one might be inclined to refute such views quite strongly. Consequently, the language surrounding the sin of humankind was not as harshly damning as it might have been.

The key to understanding human nature, even in its "fallen state," for these thinkers (among whom one might name Irenaeus of Lyons, Athanasius, Gregory of Nyssa, and Gregory of Nazianzus) lies with the problem of the body and the soul. On this particular theological locus, two main alternatives were possible: traducianism and creationism.[2] Traducianism, in general, names the idea that just as the material human body of each offspring has its origin in the material bodies of its parents in the forms of semen and egg, so too does the soul in the offspring find its origins in the particular parental souls.

According to this view, if the parents' souls were defective, so too would be the offspring's. The other approach is called creationism. This view holds that God creates a new soul for each conceived child, and that the body is then "ensouled" at conception. Augustine seems to have equivocated on his position on the matter, at times appearing to affirm traducianism,[3] and at others seeming to affirm creationism.[4] Even though, as we shall see, traducianism would be far kinder to the view of original sin Augustine later takes, he is not wholly persuaded of its dogmatic truth and thus refrains from deciding. Whichever of the main theories (or subsets thereof) one held, it was clear that the defective status of the offspring of Adam was to be taken practically as a given.

Many suppose that Augustine's understanding of original sin came out of thin air, that before him no one had held such a view. Nothing could be further from the truth. Saint Anthony, one of the "desert monks" who devoted their lives to an earthly quest to rid themselves of lust and sin, actually held to a form of original sin, albeit one that he tried to square with a robust notion of human free will.[5] Other early monks, such as Matoes and Longinus, went even further than did Anthony. They described "passions" that completely overtook the soul from birth, leading to a weakening of the soul itself.[6] Another influential early monk, Abba Moses the Black, used the image of a man carrying a sack full of sand which, unbeknownst to the carrier, has a small hole in it. "My sins run out behind me, and I do not see them."[7] Moses told this story in connection to a man about to be tried for some sin or another, and those present understood that they could not stand in judgment of sin, since all had committed sins "but could not see them." The defender of trinitarian doctrine, Athanasius, also frequently resorted to language of the primordial insatiability for sin found in the human will. While still, in some sense, free, the will as Athanasius understood it has been corrupted by its surroundings and "tends" toward sin.[8] Writing in the western strongholds of early Christianity, Tertullian could refer, without explaining exactly what he meant, to Adam as "the originator of our race *and our sin*."[9] Likewise, Cyprian of Carthage justified the practice of infant baptism by stating that the sin of the child about to be baptized had to be forgiven, this having come from "being born of the flesh according to Adam" whereby they had contracted "the contagion of the ancient death."[10] So while it is true that Augustine gave decisive weight and shape to the idea that the sin of Adam is borne as guilt and disease by all later humans, it is too much to say that he came up with original sin on his own. In fact, his elaboration of the doctrine depended heavily on these views described above, and further had much to do with the particular circumstances of his fascinating life story, to which we now turn.

AUGUSTINE OF HIPPO

Augustine was born in the Roman province of North Africa, in a town called Tagaste, in 354. His parents were of different religious persuasions; Monica, his mother, became a Christian saint, and Patricius, his father, remained a follower of traditional Roman religion (often called, condescendingly, "pagan"). Of his mother Augustine later wrote, "She earnestly endeavored, my God, that you, rather than he, should be my father."[11] Eager for their obviously gifted son to climb the social ladder of the Empire, Augustine's parents invested heavily in his education. He learned classical rhetoric and became a skilled orator. While he did show significant promise in advancing professionally, Augustine never quite fit in, either among the learned elite or among the people of his homeland. He did not know the Berber language spoken by most of his North African neighbors, and yet at the end of Augustine's long and distinguished life his cultured opponent Julian of Eclanum could dismiss him as "that African."[12]

When Augustine was a teenager, his father was unable for some time to pay for school for the young man, and Augustine bided his time by hanging around with some friends. One night, with nothing else to do, the boys sneaked in to a neighbor's field and stole some pears from a tree there. His critics have sometimes derided the hyperactive conscience Augustine shows in relating the story of how deeply this "sin" pained him. His account of the episode does, after all, fill up several pages of his *Confessions*. But what bothered Augustine was not *that* or *what* he had stolen, but *why* he had stolen. As he later came to realize, horrified, Augustine writes, "Our real pleasure was simply in doing something that was not allowed . . . The evil was foul, and I loved it; I loved destroying myself; I loved my sin—not the thing for which I had committed the sin, but the sin itself."[13]

Before long, Augustine was enamored of sins much more interesting than stealing pears. At school again in Carthage, he fell in love with falling in love. Though a man with professional ambitions like those of Augustine's would not want to marry too young, and thus be distracted from his studies and work, Augustine nonetheless found much time to spend with a variety of women. He may have later, from the perspective of an intense and chaste piety, overremembered how much he succumbed "to the flesh"; still, it is clear that he lived intemperately, and the reasons for this insatiable sexual desire drove Augustine to want to understand the origins of sin. One way Augustine came to understand sin and evil was through Manichaeism. Mani was a third century Persian prophet and philosopher who founded a religion that spread rapidly throughout the Near Eastern world. Manichaeism is fundamentally syncretistic; it combines a belief in Jesus Christ as "savior" with a quasi-Buddhist understanding of ascetic monks, has Gnostic elements among its doctrines, and gathers insights from a variety of other Persian and ancient Near Eastern religions, as well. Its central tenet was a dualism of good and evil. The world we inhabit is so obviously bereft of perfect goodness, but simultaneously so obviously lovely in some ways, that the only way to account for the copresence of good and evil is to posit two deities. One is the principle of the good, which created spirits, and the other the principle of evil, which created the material world. Since Manicheans made much of the role of stars in discerning one's fate, they were very drawn to astronomy and other forms of science. Augustine, with his rationalistic bent and his drive to understand human evil, was quickly drawn in to the Manichean religion.

He did not stay there, however. When the Manicheans were not blaming the stars for the evil humans did, they blamed their bodies. Augustine found this as finally unconvincing as he found it initially attractive. In search of another way of viewing the world, Augustine turned then to Platonism. With its vision of the body as the prison house of the soul, its celebration of reason, and a robust understanding of the soul, Platonism was a comfortable home for Augustine. He imbibed its teachings and began to wonder if they were not, after all, somehow compatible with the old faith of his mother. Platonism could explain evil (as a privation—the turning away from the higher things and toward the lower things), and did not require that Augustine give up on the rigors of the intellectual life. Yet he also thought of the Platonists he knew as people who could see a great city on the opposite shore, but lacked any way of getting across the water.[14] An explanation of evil was not enough; Augustine required a *solution*.

After Augustine's next move, the pieces all fell together. He went to Milan to teach rhetoric, and there met, in one person, the confluence of many significant patterns of thought. The man was Ambrose, bishop of Milan. A skilled orator, he appealed to Augustine's appreciation of the Ciceronian heritage. A gifted philosopher, he could relate lofty Platonic teachings to everyday experience.[15] And as a committed Christian, Ambrose showed Augustine a way to affirm the truth of the gospel in a way that spoke to his need to understand sin, evil, and redemption. Augustine became a Christian.

Quite unexpectedly and even against his will, he also became a priest, and then a bishop in the North African city of Hippo. Thus a new chapter in Augustine's life begins, one that focuses not so much on the experience and understanding of sin, but rather on the fight to define and defend the doctrines of sin and grace. For the latter of that pair, Augustine had to quarrel with the Donatists. During the great Roman persecutions of Christians, some priests had turned "apostate" and participated in Bible burnings and pagan sacrifices. Certain Christians (in some cases followers of a usurping bishop Donatus Magnus, and thus "Donatists") became persuaded that such actions eroded priestly authority so much that the sacraments performed by these priests, including baptisms, ordinations, and marriages, were invalid. Augustine labored intensely to arrive at a doctrine of grace, and of the church, that could answer such questions. His answer came in two forms, the second of which has a most direct bearing on this chapter's focus on original sin. First, since there is "one holy, catholic and apostolic church" and since there were in most North African cities two competing bishops—one Donatist and one, for lack of a better term, Roman—one of the groups must be in error. Since the Donatists were in communion only with each other, and the Romans with all other churches throughout the empire, Augustine reasoned that the Donatists must be the schismatics. But secondly, and more importantly, Augustine saw the practical, pastoral need that people be able to rely on the efficacy and validity of sacraments in the church. Further, Augustine was persuaded that *all had sinned*, and thus it did not make sense to assert that the consequences of the particular priestly sin of cooperation with a persecuting empire should be so much graver than any other sin.

Augustine's notion of sin comes to a head in the other great theological confrontation of his life, the Pelagian controversy. Pelagius was a British monk who, after visiting Rome, the center of his religion and object of his previously distant admiration, was appalled at the low moral standards he observed there. He read with horror Augustine's statement in the Confessions, "Give me, O God, what you command, and command whatever you wish."[16] Such a sentiment seemed to make humans robots to be manipulated by a capricious God, and Pelagius would have none of it. He responded by teaching that God expected moral perfection of human beings, and would not expect it if it were not possible. Once maximal exertion had been expended, God's grace effected a reunion of the sinner with God in blessedness. To reduce a complicated position to its simplest level, one might say that Pelagius taught that God helped those who helped themselves. Nothing could be further from Augustine's own experience, however, and from his understanding of the gospel. Indeed, as he himself later stated, "God helps those who *cannot* help themselves."[17]

WHAT AUGUSTINE SAID

Augustine had his basic theological anthropology worked out well in advance of the theological crisis with Pelagius that led to his development of the doctrine of original sin. It is characterized first by an extremely rosy picture of how all humans were intended to be in their created nature, and how Adam and Eve, before the fall, actually were. Adam was possessed of "original righteousness," meaning that he acted justly in every way. He was not subject to sickness of body or of mind.[18] He was intellectually superior to all the creatures around him, to say nothing of those fallen humans who came after him.[19] It was conceivable, so Augustine thought, that Adam and Eve might have been spared from an earthly death, if they could have continued to be nourished from the rich fruit of Eden's gardens.[20] Since sin is, for Augustine, always an act of the will, it is perhaps most important to note that Adam's *will* was ideal in every way possible. Augustine made a distinction between the "ability not to sin" and the "inability to sin." The former (in Latin, *posse non peccare*) was the sort of thing that Adam had, and the latter (in Latin, *non posse peccare*) was the sort of thing that all might hope to experience in the blessedness that lies hereafter.[21] By asserting that Adam had the freedom not to sin, Augustine meant that his will was properly ordered. Following Plato once again, Augustine thought that the will was naturally created to want the better things of the world *more*. A human will, acting according to its created nature, will always prefer eternal love to fleeting romance, steak to dog food, and excellence to mediocrity in all things. Such a will would, therefore, naturally prefer to obey God's just commandments than to disobey them.[22] When Adam contradicts this inclination to the good that God has given him, he is acting out of his creatureliness. Since he is a temporal creature, not eternal creator, Adam was susceptible to change, and thus potentially inclined to turn away from eternal goods for momentary pleasures.[23] That he should not have done this is obvious, and the senselessness of his fall is highlighted by Augustine's insistence that God had given Adam the special gift of perseverance in willing the good.[24] As Augustine contemplates the sheer unlikeliness that Adam would trade in such clear blessedness for such lousy perversion, he is at a loss. God had given Adam every advantage, and the only prohibition on his life was for Adam's own good.[25] In fact, Augustine once wrote (and keep in mind that this is coming from a person who wrote a magnificent book on the mystery of the Trinity), "Nothing is so impenetrable to the understanding" and yet so central to the Christian faith than this ancient sin.[26]

What is clear to Augustine is that pride rested at the root of that first sin. Adam wanted to place himself, rather than his creator, at the center of his world. He chose to have knowledge of good and evil, heretofore a possession of God's alone, and Augustine makes clear that absent this pride (Augustine's word is *superbia*), he would never have listened to Eve or the serpent.[27] Though to the average reader Adam's transgression of freedom by eating of the fruit forbidden by God might not seem so terrible, Augustine reminds us that we can't compare Adam's actions to ours, since our freedom is so diminished. Adam was really, truly free, and his departure from that pristine freedom is utterly *sui generis* and, practically speaking, inexplicable.[28]

Two aspects of Augustine's formulation of the doctrine of original sin need to be highlighted at this point. The first is the nature of later humankind's *responsibility* for original sin, and the second is its *effects*. Augustine repeatedly makes statements like, "We were all one in Adam when he sinned."[29] Since we are all partakers of the same human nature, Augustine thinks he can meaningfully say that all sinned in Adam's action. "All then sinned in Adam, when in his nature, by virtue of that innate power whereby he was able to produce them [his descendants], they were all as yet the one Adam; but they are called *another's*, because as yet they were not living their own lives, but the life of the one man contained whatsoever was in his future posterity."[30] In other words, since Adam and all his later descendents shared the same human nature, and since what was latent in Adam is actual in us, one can meaningfully say that "Adam sinned" and "I sinned" are essentially equivalent statements. Human nature rebelled against God, and Augustine is little concerned about which particular wearer of the one human nature is guiltiest.[31]

Now on to the second feature of Augustine's account of original sin. The rhetorically gifted bishop does not mince words when describing the *effects* that inherited original sin has on all descendants of Adam. It is important to note that, however strongly Augustine thinks that Adam's sin has weakened human nature, the human creature is still fundamentally good. "Since 'man placed in honor fell; he has become like the beasts,' and generates [reproduces] as they do, though the little spark of reason, which was the image of God in him, has not been quite quenched."[32] Or elsewhere, "Even the fallen soul remains God's image"[33] and is "capable of knowing God."[34] The human will has been weakened, corrupted, made perverse, and become distorted, but it is not nonexistent. Indeed, Augustine can still affirm a kind of "freedom of the will." But the freedom that it now displays is just corrupt, weak, and perverse enough to continue to choose sin freely.[35]

The last feature of Augustine's notion of original sin—perhaps the best known and most widely discredited one—is its propagation. Augustine links the transmission of the contagion of sin and its guilt (for Augustine employs both medical and juridical metaphors to describe sin's taint[36]) to the act of procreation. In its original, intended state, the act of sex was bereft of any inordinate, intemperate lustful desire, or concupiscence. Sex was experienced as good because it resulted in the fruitfulness of the generations. After the fall, when Adam and Eve become aware of their nakedness and their wills begin to war against reason, they give us a hint at the nature of the fault. Augustine is quick to pick up on it. They cover their sex organs with fig leaves.[37] As Peter Brown imagines the scene, Augustine says, from the pulpit, "*Ecce unde*! That's the place! That's the place from which the first sin is passed on!"[38] Sexual impulse, as we now feel it, distracts us from the higher things we ought to contemplate more and governs our thoughts to an inordinate degree.[39] It was a pervasive, ineradicable imprisonment of the human mind and will, and spread itself and its deleterious effects by the sexual act.[40]

WHY AUGUSTINE SAID IT

Many have disapproved of Augustine over the years for having focused so heavily on human misery and the capacity, even proclivity, of humans to sin. He has been criticized for making central to Christian life the understanding of death, and of being so aware of his own supposed lust that he had little positive to say about human bodiliness at all. Some of these criticisms have their merit, but some caution should be exercised when looking at the unrelentingly hardheaded nature of Augustine's doctrine. His context, after all, is important for understanding what he meant.

For example, Augustine was bishop in Hippo, in what is now northern Algeria, and by all accounts it was a very difficult place to live. Deadly plagues were common, and Augustine was frequently asked to pray for the physical healing of his parishioners. Life expectancies were low, and life was, in general, dangerous. Heavy taxation, required for keeping the delicate Roman peace intact, placed immense burdens on ordinary people. In this context it would make no sense, pastorally speaking, to praise the goodness of the body, disease-ridden as most were, or sing songs of praise to the wonders of created matter. Indeed, to espouse teachings in that way would have been pastorally cruel. Little wonder that Augustine sought to meet his parishioners' real experiences of bodily pain. But the real key to understanding *why* Augustine affirmed a teaching of original sin has to do with another pastoral matter: the practice of baptizing infants.

By the end of the fourth century, it was standard practice in all Christian churches to baptize infants. An ecumenical council put into writing what was already widely believed when the Nicene creed stated that "We acknowledge one baptism for the forgiveness of sins."[41] If a child was baptized, then, it must be for the forgiveness of sins. And since it was not for future sins about to be committed, the logic ran, the child must be sinful. While this can sound odd to us, such a sentiment actually accorded with Augustine's own experience. A child that has had plenty to eat, Augustine noted, still looks at his nursing brother with contempt and jealousy. Who are we to say that such a one is without sin?[42] Further, infant baptisms were often performed in the context of exorcisms and somber renunciations of the devil and his work.[43] So Augustine reasons, at least partially, from cure to diagnosis, rather than the other way round, as is often assumed. Since forgiveness of sins *is conferred* in baptism, then the baptized (though it be an infant) must have the stain of sin upon it—QED.

TAKING THE FALL SERIOUSLY, OR HISTORICALLY?

For many hundreds of years the doctrine of original sin had a special kind of persuasive weight because virtually all Christians, including Christian theologians, understood the sins of Adam and Eve to be events in history, such that their effects would be historically felt by their descendants. The Garden of Eden was understood to be a physical place, and the transgressions of the first couple were actual events a few thousand years ago, after which humans were expelled from paradise. This view began to be challenged in the eighteenth and nineteenth centuries, for a variety of reasons. First, as Christians began to be more sophisticated in their approaches to reading the Bible, it did not make sense to try to make everything in the text equally "historical." That is, some texts seem to be intended to be read as histories, and some not.[44] Second, modern science began to produce evidence that humans have been on Earth for much longer than we might suppose if we took the Bible as a quasi-scientific and "historical" source for human origins. Early church fathers, among them St. Augustine, calculated based on genealogies in the Old Testament that Adam and Eve were created around 5509 BC.[45] If we read the Bible in this way, what are we to make of the fact that scientists date human existence at least as far back as 250,000 and 400,000 BC?[46]

The answer to that question involves some of the most serious, and intemperate, theological debates of the last 150 years. In examining the literature, it has become apparent, at least to me, that no necessary conflict needs to exist between the creation and fall stories of Genesis 1–4 and modern science. Those who assert that the only way to read the Bible is as a sourcebook of history, "inerrant" with respect to what a critical historian would say about the events it describes, seem to me to be misguided. To compare the Bible (written between 3000 and 1900 years ago) with critical history (a discipline not really developed until 300 years ago), in order to show the superiority of the former, does not make sense.

Further, attention to the texts in Genesis allows us to see that the writers there did not necessarily intend for all readers to take the texts historically. For example, the name they give to the first human is "Adam." Now, the word "Adam" simply means "man." If I were going to write a story about events long, long ago, and I did *not* want my readers to take the story literally, naming the central character simply "man" would be a good clue as to my intentions. In fact, the whole first 11 chapters of Genesis seem to be written in this way. The intent of the authors seems to be to distance the world they describe from the world we inhabit. People live for hundreds and hundreds of years. Animals talk to humans. Divine creatures engage in sexual intercourse with human females. When Adam and Eve's son Cain is held accountable for murdering his brother Abel, he is sent to go live in the city of Nod, where he takes a wife. Yet as far as we know from the text, Adam, Eve, and Cain are the only people around![47] Christians have long noted that whereas "day" seems to refer to the period of one evening and one morning in the first creation story (Gen. 1.1–28), just a few verses later it refers to an undisclosed length of time (Gen. 2.4b). A land populated with talking animals (Gen. 3.1–5) and people who live to be hundreds and hundreds of years old (e.g. Gen. 5.27), and where angel-like creatures seduce and copulate with human females (Gen. 6.4) virtually cries out to be interpreted in a nonhistorical way that honors the great divide between the world so imagined therein and the world the reader occupies.

ORIGINAL SIN AND ITS "WAGES": DEATH

Another difficulty besetting those who wish to appropriate the doctrine of original sin for our own time, in addition to its apparent dependence on a woodenly literal reading of Genesis, is its linkage with death. If not for original sin, would none have died? The thought is so foreign to our ordinary understandings that it can scarcely be right. Yet the Apostle Paul writes, in the context of his discussion of the righteousness lost in Adam and restored in Christ, a famous statement about sin. "Now that you have been freed from sin and enslaved to God, the advantage you get is sanctification. The end is eternal life. For the wages of sin is death, but the free gift of God is eternal life in Christ Jesus our Lord."[48] The wages of sin is death. That Paul thinks of death here as a consequence of sin is clear, and that this sin-death linkage is traceable to the first transgression in the Garden of Eden is a reasonable inference from Paul's argument. What are we to make of that? Can we really say that human nature, as created by God, was not originally intended to include death? Did death enter the picture of human reality only after Adam and Eve's fall from grace?[49]

To affirm that position would be very difficult. Since human beings are finite creatures of an infinite God, the fact that our earthly lives have an end seems somewhat "natural" to most of us. It is difficult to imagine earthly existence as finite creatures who did not die. The fact that I will, eventually, die gives meaning to my choices. I cannot choose to prepare myself for thousands of different careers, since I only have a few decades to work.[50] I do not have time to test out one after another in a string of serious, long-term romantic relationships. The fact that I will die contributes to, in a sense, rather than diminishes, the goodness of human lives. Then again, the reality of death at the end of life can also seem to encourage sin. Let us continue the examples of work and romantic relationships used above. Since I have to choose a single career (or a small number of them) the pressure is on to succeed in that career. This pressure might motivate me to, say, overreport my performance, or try to make myself look better at the expense of my colleagues, or cheat in some way to get ahead. And the fact that traditional monogamous relationships can feel, at times, restrictive often leads to adultery and betrayal. So there is a kind of connection between sin and death, to be sure. It is worth noting, however, that what seems most important is *how* we each deal with the reality of death, rather than death itself.

When Paul links sin and death together, he does not consistently mean *physical* death. For example, in Ephesians Paul addresses physically living persons by saying "You were dead through the trespasses and sins in which you once lived, following the ruler of the power of the air . . . "[51] And when Paul asserts that "the sting of death is sin" in 1 Corinthians 15.56, he is speaking in a Christological context. There he means that, given Christ's resurrection, we can see that death is incidental to human nature, even if an earthly death awaits all who possess such a nature. Paul may well have been following a long-established rabbinic style of interpretation that did, in fact, attribute the reality of death to Adam's sin. The Wisdom of Solomon (in the biblical Apocrypha, or Intertestamental literature), for example, states that "God creates us for incorruption, and made us in the image of his own eternity, but through the devil's envy death entered the world, and those who belong to his company experience it."[52]

Still, on the whole, it seems as though the biblical writings assume that there is nothing, per se, wrong with a finite life span.[53] When the heroes of the Hebrew Bible live long and prosperous lives, richly enjoying the blessings of family and faith, and then die in the presence of their loved ones, content with a life well lived, we do not draw the inference that such a death must be evil. Rather, it is the extreme *fear of death* that creates problems. If fear of death frustrates any risk taking, any openness to vulnerability, then it closes us off from life and keeps us from living at all. As we shall see in the next chapter, this kind of closed-off-ness to life and its relationships is certainly connected to sin. To this extent, then, (and perhaps no further), drawing a connection between sin and death seems proper and instructive.

BLAMING THE VICTIM?

Over the centuries, readers of Genesis and exponents of original sin have been quick to point out a detail of the Garden of Eden story. They note that it was Eve who sinned "first" and then persuaded her husband to follow in defying God's commandment not to eat of the fruit of the tree of the knowledge of good and evil. By this one datum have heaps and heaps of judgments denigrating women been justified. Consider the following sampler platter, arranged from the great buffet of sexist theological reflection in the Christian tradition. Irenaeus of Lyons (d. 202 AD), the influential Christian bishop in the second century of the church, wrote that "Having become disobedient, [Eve] was made the cause of death, both to herself and to the entire human race." [54] From the third century we could cite Origen (d. 254 AD), brilliant theologian in northern Africa, who wrote, "What is seen with the eyes of the creator is masculine, and not feminine, for God does not stoop to look upon what is feminine and of the flesh." [55] A fourth century exemplar could be Ambrose (d. 397), the great bishop in Milan, who argued, "Eve was first to be deceived and was responsible for deceiving the man." [56] In the fifth century, though we could dish up from many sources, consider this grossly blunt statement about Eve from John of Chrysostom (d. 407): "The woman taught once, and ruined all." [57] It would not be difficult to continue this exercise, because an extraordinary amount of blame for all kinds of consequences of later sin has been attributed to Eve's first transgression, and the disdain and contempt that such blame placing arouses has been transferred to women in general.

Even so brief a history as this reminds us that we need to be especially careful in reasserting and reinterpreting the doctrine of original sin, so that the victim of its abuses is not continually blamed. Some feminist theologians have recently tried to construct a notion of sin that takes women's needs and experiences seriously, some of whom go back to Eden for guidance. Susan Dunfee, for example, notes that

Eve's sin is not so much willful self-assertion (pride) as it is *hiding*. Adam and Eve hide from God when they realize their sin, and historically many women have been content with too little, not exercising their powers and rights strongly enough in the public sphere.[58] As we will see in the next chapter, Karl Barth calls this the sin of "sloth." Yet when reexaminations of the fall stories in Genesis lead to an essentialization of supposedly "feminine" characteristics, or when the aim of such examinations becomes the transference of blame from one character to another, we know that we have gone off track.

"IN ADAM'S FALL, WE SINNED ALL"

Perhaps the single most important assertion made by the doctrine of original sin is the fellowship of humanity that it assumes. The quotation at the top of this chapter from Chesterton bears repeating: "Christianity preaches an obviously unattractive idea, such as original sin; but when we wait for its results, they are pathos and brotherhood and a thunder of laughter and pity; for only with original sin can we at once pity the beggar and distrust the king." The influential Yale University chaplain and civil rights activist William Sloane Coffin remarked, "If we are not yet joined to one another in love, we most surely are in sin, and sin is a wonderful bond because it precludes the possibility of separation through judgment."[59] But how does this "bond" exist? What connects someone born in the present day not only to all other humans in her midst, but also to Adam, Eve, and all their "progeny"?

Schoolchildren in New England in colonial days were taught their ABCs by the use of a helpful tool that linked memorable couplets to the letters of the alphabet. "E" was for "Elijah hid, by Ravens fed." "J" was for "Job feels the rod, yet blesses God." My personal favorite is "Q," which is "Queen Esther sues, and saves the Jews." More importantly for our purposes, however, is the letter "A," which stood for "In Adam's fall, we sinned all."[60] When Adam sinned, the sentiment seems to go, he did not sin alone, for you and I sinned then, too. The idea strikes our twenty-first century ear funnily. Many of us have been blamed for doing things we did not do, but to be blamed for something done thousands of years before we were born? How could people in the eighteenth century believe such a thing?

The greatest American theologian of this time period (or of any time period, for that matter) is instructive for seeing how such thought patterns were possible, and, if we were willing, how they might be recovered. This would be Jonathan Edwards. Edwards wrote a book called, simply, *Original Sin*, in which he defends the traditional notion in the face of advances in science and philosophy in his day. When Augustine was trying to explain how future generations were responsible for original sin, he used the philosophy most widely known at his own time—Platonism, or more accurately, Neoplatonism. Plato taught that everything that existed in the temporal, tangible world of our experiences was a concrete expression of abstract "ideas" or "forms." This means that every human person is a concrete example of an abstract "ideal" human person. So when Adam sinned, all who share his "ideal"—namely, all other people—are complicit. Edwards took a different approach. He also used the cutting edge philosophy of his time to help explain his view on how "in Adam's fall, we sinned all." That philosophy is known as empiricism. Empiricists believe that the way the human mind thinks about a thing contributes, in part, to the reality of that thing. The great empirical philosopher and Irish bishop George Berkeley (d. 1783) gave a helpful slogan to this way of thinking. "To be is to be perceived." Thus the way God thinks about humans, such as two as apparently different as Adam and the author of this book, contributes to their reality. Edwards thinks that individual persons should not, in fact, be treated as "discrete entities." We know that this is true because we refer to a man as the same person at 60 as he was as an infant, even though his entire body has changed.[61] Such personal continuity through time and space is due to the providential way that God "thinks" about us. Take another example. Sometimes I might think of my arm as one distinct thing, and my leg as another distinct thing. But at other times I might think of them both as "parts" of my body, and thus basically equivalent. Neither view is necessarily "wrong." Both are possible, and what matters is the purpose to which such thinking is directed.[62] Applying this empiricist logic to personal identity vis-à-vis Adam and other humans, Edwards writes, "God, in each step of his proceeding with Adam, in relation to the covenant or constitution established with him, looked on his posterity as being *one with him*."[63] Therefore, according to this logic, it does not really make sense to protest that it is unfair that we are punished for the sin of another. Seen from God's point of view, humanity is, and humans are, one.

If it does nothing else, original sin helps us to see the bonds of fellowship and the universal need for grace such a plight entails. The miners rescued from a months-long imprisonment in the San Jose mine in Chile developed a closeness few will ever experience. There is a kind of esprit de corps that runs through people who know their connection to others in mutual suffering and misery. Those who wish to cast off original sin as a vestige of an irrational epoch, or as corrosive of moral exertion, or as scientifically disreputable, pious mumbling, must consider the power with which it displays, as Alan Jacobs puts it, "the confraternity of the human type."[64]

CHAPTER 4

SIN-NONYMS: ESTRANGEMENT, ISOLATION, REBELLION, AND SELF-JUSTIFICATION

If the death of Christ be our redemption, then we were captives; if it be satisfaction, we were debtors; if it be atonement, we were guilty; if it be cleansing, we were unclean.
> —John Calvin, *Commentary on Galatians and Ephesians (on Gal. 2.21)*

A God without wrath brought men without sin into a Kingdom without judgment through the ministrations of a Christ without a cross.
> —H. Richard Niebuhr, lampooning "liberal" theology's supposed inattention to sin in *The Kingdom of God in America*

Sin is not confined to the evil things we do. It is the evil within us, the evil which we are. Shall we call it our pride or our laziness, or shall we call it the deceit of our life? Let us call it for once the great defiance which turns us again and again into the enemies of God and of our fellowmen, even of our own selves.
> —Karl Barth, *Deliverance to the Captives*

We have thus far been discussing "sin" as though it has meant just one thing in Christian theological history. Nothing could be further from the truth, however. All manner of different words have been suggested as clarifiers for what is meant by the Christian word sin.[1] If the reader will allow a terrible pun, we could refer to these as "sin-nonyms." Though it would be possible to align dozens of different synonyms for sin side by side, this chapter lays out four different ones: sin as estrangement, sin as isolation, sin as rebellion, and sin as self-justification. For each sin-nonym, a brief analysis of the concept is offered, followed by an exegesis of a biblical passage the concept seeks to illumine, and a discussion of an influential contemporary thinker who has made use of the concept in articulating a fuller understanding of sin. What is highlighted in some proposals for how to construe sin is diminished in others. What is central to one philosophical underpinning to a theological doctrine of sin is peripheral to another. Thus the juxtaposition of these four schema side by side will aid us in evaluating what the advantages and shortcomings are of these several approaches to sin.

ACTING OTHER THAN BEING: SIN AS ESTRANGEMENT

"He's just not himself today."
"I can't believe that she did that—it's so unlike her."

Phrases like this speak to a divide between how, and who, we understand ourselves to be and how and who we actually sometimes are. Theologians have often called this divide sin. More specifically, a word that speaks to how sin makes us be unlike our true selves is *estrangement*. The great Christian ethicist Stanley Hauerwas once cleverly entitled an article in a way that helps us see that persons as they essentially are, and persons as they actually are, can be estranged from one another. The essay is called, "Must a Patient Be a Person to Be a Patient? Or, My Uncle Charlie Is Not Much of a Person, but He Is Still My Uncle Charlie."[2] To get the joke of the title is to have in mind, simultaneously, that we know what it truly means to be a "person" and that Uncle Charlie, whoever he is, doesn't quite measure up to the standard. That doesn't mean that Uncle Charlie doesn't count, somehow. It just means that, like the rest of us, he falls short of what he was intended to be. He is "estranged" from something. We might even say that he is estranged from his true self.

Consider the words "essential" and "existential." To make clearer the ways in which we are estranged from ourselves and from God in sin, we can think about our essential selves and our existential selves. Essential refers, of course, to the innermost purity of a thing. It belongs to the essence of ice that it is cold, to fire that it is hot, and so on. One's "essential self" is who one is when acting as one was truly intended to be. As difficult as this might be to nail down, the fact that people know when they are not acting "like themselves" implies that we have some access to this essential self. The existential self is the one that exists from day to day. The word "exist" comes from *exsistere*, which means to stand or to step out of. We step out of the timeless eternity of essences and have to live in the everyday world of existence. When things come up in everyday existence, like deadlines that make us anxious, or relationships that make us tense, or tragedies that make us depressed, our existential selves act out of line with our essential selves. This is not only the occasion for sin, but also a cause of sin. It seems most honest to say that our "true" selves comprise both their existential and essential dimensions. The "real" incorporates both the ideal and the actual into itself.[3]

Illustrative exegesis: Romans 7.14–25

For a closer look at how this dynamic plays out in religious terms, we could turn to the Apostle Paul's description of human nature in Romans 7. Here Paul presents what is sometimes called "the inner conflict." By appealing to Paul's account to illustrate what I mean, I do not imply that Paul has in mind terms like "essential" and "existential" selfhood. To say that would be sheer anachronism. But Paul understands the simultaneity of the practical need for the law of God in everyday living and also its deeper purpose and nature. In Romans 7.14–25 we read,

> For we know that the law is spiritual; but I am of the flesh, sold into slavery under sin. I do not understand my own actions. For I do not do what I want, but I do the very thing I hate. Now if I do what I do not want, I agree that the law is good. But in fact it is no longer I that do it, but sin that dwells within me. For I know that nothing good dwells within me, that is, in my flesh. I can will what is right, but I cannot do it. For I do not do the good I want, but the evil I do not want is what I do. Now if I do what I do not want, it is no longer I that do it, but sin that dwells within me. So I find it to be a law that when I want to do what is good, evil lies close at hand. For I delight in the law of God in my inmost self, but I see in my members another law at war with the law of my mind, making me captive to the law of sin that dwells in my members. Wretched man that I am! Who will rescue me from this body of death? Thanks be to God through Jesus Christ our Lord![4]

Sentences like "I do not do what I want, but I do the very thing I hate" are difficult to understand. They can be made clearer if we think of sin as estrangement. "I (existential self) do not do what I (essential self) want, but I (existential self) do the very thing that I (essential self) hate. I (essential self) can will what is right, but I (existential self) cannot do it. The law of God is a delight to the inmost self (the essential self, clearly), but in reality, the law becomes for Paul an oppressive reminder of how he falls short in daily life to the expectations and standards of God.[5] In sin we are not ourselves. We are estranged from God—made nearly unrecognizable, but not quite—and estranged from ourselves. Salvation will thus be understood as reunion with the basis of our essence, and an overcoming of the distance between us as we are and us as we were meant to be.

Exemplary modern thinker: Paul Tillich

Paul Tillich (1886–1965) is an example of a recent theologian who has made use of the category of estrangement to elucidate the doctrine of sin.[6] Tillich, as much a philosopher as a theologian, was preoccupied with questions of ontology, or the concepts of "being." Existence is simply being as we experience it, which involves "standing out" of essences. This act of standing out of the comfort of timelessness then entails a kind of distance from our essential nature.[7]

To know what this means we have to look at Tillich's most general account of what it is for a human "to be." For Tillich, every encounter that the human being has with the world has roughly the same shape, and it consists in a set of "polar structures."[8] Every human event requires us, first, to find a balance between "individuation" and "participation." Each person is different, unique, and yet we are not so dissimilar from one another that the classification "human" makes no sense. Millions of people speak English (participation), but none speaks it exactly like another (individuation). Each wants to love and be loved, but no one's beloved or sources of love are exactly the same as those of someone else. Problems ensue when either of these two poles—or ends of a continuum—is inordinately favored.

Secondly, there is the polar pair of "freedom and destiny." Humans interact with the world according to their will, since we each have some measure of freedom. But freedom is never infinite. All kinds of factors limit the freedom of our actions. We have developed patterns of habit and trajectories of decision making. When we exercise our freedom to, say, conceive and raise a child, the fact that we now have a child constrains our freedom in all kinds of ways obvious to everyone who is a parent.[9] All those factors that limit freedom Tillich lumps under freedom's polar partner "destiny." He means this not in the sense of a fatalistic determinism wherein nothing new can happen. Rather, destiny means for Tillich that lives unfold along certain trajectories, where at least some events are expected. In our culture there is a kind of social norm (though by no means a universally accepted one) that young people attend school, then move away from home, then "settle down" with someone, and so forth. That is not the pattern for all people, obviously, but it is a kind of "destiny" in that it is a trajectory along which many people meaningfully exercise their freedom.

Thirdly, there is the polar pair of "dynamism and form." Each day, we wake up to certain things having stayed the same since we went to sleep. Grammatical rules haven't changed, the basic personalities of our friends haven't changed. Tillich refers to this dimension of human being as "form." On the other hand, every day new words, phrases, and sentences are created using those same old formal rules. Every day new conversations and new experiences happen between those same old friends. To this dimension of being, characterized by novelty and creativity, Tillich gives the name "dynamism."

If human being is the sum total of all these polar tensions—individualization and participation, freedom and destiny, dynamism and form—then the human is in trouble. Each of these pairs tends to fall apart. We cannot manage the perfect balance ourselves. In other words, the human risks falling victim to *nonbeing*. Nonbeing threatens us daily with the specter of dissolution. Asserting one pole completely, and allowing the other to recede fully, leaves us broken and vulnerable. This transition from essence to existence is not a moment in time. Rather, it is a kind of metaphor. Tillich uses the *symbol* of the Fall to describe it. Essential humanity is like a "dreaming innocence" which is created, and therefore not God, yet does not have to "stand out" of itself into all the vicissitudes and threats of the world of existence.[10] When the essential human steps out into existence, the result is a "fall," but not in such a way that the human existent has no connection to its essential forebear. As Tillich puts it, "The fall is not a break [from the essential realm], but an imperfect fulfillment."[11]

Thus under the conditions of existence, sin will be everywhere around us and in us. We will overassert ourselves as individuals or shrink away from what is demanded of us. We will try to overcome our limitations by the raw exercise of freedom, or we will refuse to resist the deadly trajectories of those around us. The poles *will* fall apart. In Tillich's thought, it is only because the essential triune God becomes incarnate in the murkiness of existence that we have the hope that our world will not forever fall apart. Sin is estrangement, then, of our existential self from its essential forebear, and from the God who is the Ground of the Being of both.

ACTING ALONE: SIN AS ISOLATION AND RELATIONLESSNESS

Closely related to, but importantly different from, estrangement is the concept of relationlessness. Estrangement is the internal distance one has from one's true nature. Isolation is the refusal to be connected to that which fosters and secures one's true nature. To be human is always to be *social*. The image of God in which humans are created is at its heart relational, since relationality lies at the heart of the triune God in whose image we are made. If sociality is a hallmark of authentic human being, then sin can be conceived as a rupture or negation of the life-giving interpersonal and person-God relationships that result in inauthentic human being. Human selves tend to desire to think of themselves as self-securing, autonomous, impermeable persons. To admit the degree of relationality that lies at the core of our identity takes courage. No one's sense of oneself comes without a vast matrix of social relationships that contribute to the self's identity. I cannot explain fully who I am without mentioning my wife, my parents, my friends, and so on. They are part of me. Speaking from the theological standpoint, too, in order to express relatively adequately who I am, I would have to make some kind of mention of God, in relationship to whom my primary identity is cast. To be closed off from that relationship is both a consequence of sin and sin itself. To be closed off from, or to be in distorted relationships with, those partners whom God has given me is both a consequence of sin and sin itself. To get a closer look at the specifics of this particular way of thematizing sin, we can look again at an illustrative biblical text, one whose subject is King Solomon and his sin, and an exemplary modern thinker, the contemporary Lutheran theologian Eberhard Jüngel.

Illustrative exegesis: 1 Kings 11.3–10

The great theological mind who wrote many of the prophetic books of the Old Testament is known to us as the "Deuteronomist." He wrote, not surprisingly, the book of Deuteronomy, but also Joshua, Judges, 1 and 2 Samuel, and 1 and 2 Kings.[12] These latter writings are known as the "former prophets." The texts themselves are really an interpretation of the history of Israel from the time of their servitude in Egypt through the reconquest of Palestine, the times of the judges, and the first centuries of kings in Israel and Judah. Ordinarily, we do not think of "history" as counting as "prophecy." Prophecy seems, at first glance, to be mostly a prediction of the future, whereas history concerns itself with the past. However, as was noted in Chapter 2, the way the Deuteronomist tells his story of the development of Israel and Judah speaks powerfully to the Judeans of his day and promotes a vision of the future that we could certainly understand as "prophetic."

The hero of the Deuteronomistic history and prophecy is David, whose chief virtue, among his many dozens of virtues, is his intimate connection with God. The phrase "David was *with* God" or "God was *with* David" appears over and over again.[13] David is free to ignore some of Israel's customs, and even some of God's laws, because of this close, intimate relationship with God. For example, David and his men are permitted to eat the "bread of the presence" taken from the temple at Nob. Ordinarily only the priest, in this case Ahimelech, would be allowed to consume such bread (1 Sam. 21.1–6). But David's close connection with God obviates such strictures. Likewise, when David's first son by Bathsheba is ailing, and then dies, David reverses the order of mourning and fasting (2 Sam. 12.15b–23). He is depicted as speaking personally and emotionally with God. Since he does so, his unorthodox way of mourning his loss is acceptable.

The foil of David in the sense of intimacy with God is his son Solomon. Although Solomon is portrayed as possessing some virtuous characteristics of his own, such as his wisdom and his energetic building activities, Solomon cannot match David in his intimacy with God. At the end of Solomon's reign, we see him sullen, withdrawn, and moving in the direction of sin. In fact, one might call his sin primarily the sin of *isolation* from God and from neighbor. Consider the following passage from 1 Kings 11.3–10:

Among his wives were seven hundred princesses and three hundred concubines; and his wives turned away his heart. For when Solomon was old, his wives turned away his heart after other gods; and his heart was not true to the Lord his God, as was the heart of his father David. For Solomon followed Astarte the goddess of the Sidonians, and Milcom the abomination of the Ammonites. So Solomon did what was evil in the sight of the Lord, and did not completely follow the Lord, as his father David had done. Then Solomon built a high place for Chemosh the abomination of Moab, and for Molech the abomination of the Ammonites, on the mountain east of Jerusalem. He did the same for all his foreign wives, who offered incense and sacrificed to their gods. Then the Lord was angry with Solomon, because his heart had turned away from the Lord, the God of Israel, who had appeared to him twice, and had commanded him concerning this matter, that he should not follow other gods; but he did not observe what the Lord commanded.

We can easily imagine Solomon here, who, since he has 700 wives and 300 concubines, can afford to not really know or spend time with any of them. He has become brooding and solitary, moving away from the relationships of love that are life-giving. The actions of Solomon that are denounced, namely, building altars for foreign gods and letting the religions of his foreign wives "pollute" the monotheistic faith that the Deuteronomist is so keen to recover, are really just symptoms. Solomon has allowed himself to be isolated. He is isolated personally, professionally, and religiously. The number of wives that Solomon has, interestingly enough, is not told in a way that invites moral judgment. From the perspective of the sexual ethics of the Deuteronomist, Solomon is not to be chastised for excessive lust. In a different sense, however, the number of wives is problematic. Instead of fighting wars to settle disputes, as his father David did, Solomon prefers to work diplomatically, often taking the daughter of a foreign king as a wife to seal his treaty with the potential enemy. Such willingness to intermingle with Israel's neighbors, all of whom were polytheistic, is the real source of concern for the Deuteronomist. Yet it is also clear that Solomon has opted, even in the presence of so many other relationships, to "go it alone." The fact that his harem is so large might imply unfaith; it might be the case that Solomon is concerned for "self-generated fertility" rather than a reliance on God for the securing of one's family and legacy.[14] David frequently consulted with advisors, prophets, and his military leaders. We do not read of such relationality in Solomon. That he has so isolated himself, in the view of the Deuteronomist, is his characteristic sin.

Exemplary modern thinker: Eberhard Jüngel

One of the great theological minds writing in recent decades is the German Lutheran theologian and philosopher of religion Eberhard Jüngel. Jüngel has written many books, but his oeuvre includes, to date, neither a complete systematic theology nor a book explicitly devoted to sin or the nature of human being. However, in a wide array of searching essays and tightly argued books, Jüngel has articulated a consistent understanding of human sin. Perhaps the word that best epitomizes Jüngel's view of sin is *relationlessness*. Much in the spirit of the foregoing exegesis of Solomon and his sin, Jüngel thinks that human persons betray their created nature by sinning first in their efforts to secure their own meaning and value, then in cutting off oneself from the relationships that bestow identity, and thirdly by denying that one's relationship with God is in fact determinative of human identity and value. We can call these three moments "self-actualization," "relationlessness as such," and "unbelief."

Beginning with the notion of self-actualization, Jüngel has repeatedly criticized the typically modern depiction of humans as *homo faber* (self-made person).[15] Productivity and self-realization exist in direct correlation to value in the modern human, such that the increase in the one is the only way to an increase in the other. In what has become something of an axiom in his writings on the matter, Jüngel satirizes the modern outlook as "without an increase in performance, no increase in quality of life."[16] The human is to forge his or her own way, according to the moderns (and Jüngel means especially here the tradition from Descartes through Gotthold Lessing and Max Scheler), relying totally on oneself both to find and to create meaning. Allow a single brief quotation to suffice: "In an almost breath-taking manner, the modern human person . . . has discovered and experienced that through our actions we increasingly become not only the measure of all things, but something even more: nothing less than the decisive authority over all things. That we 'make ourselves, as it were, into the lords and masters of nature' is, according to Descartes, precisely the goal of [modern] philosophy."[17]

One of the reasons Jüngel is insistent on taking the emphasis in anthropology totally away from the concept of activity is because he has seen where that idea goes. He repeatedly reminds us of Luther's decisive critique of Aristotle's claim in the Nicomachean Ethics that a person becomes just by doing just acts. This conception gets it exactly backwards, says Luther (and Jüngel), "For we are not, as Aristotle believes, made righteous by the doing of just deeds; . . . but rather in becoming and being righteous people we do just deeds."[18] It doesn't make any sense, Jüngel thinks, to talk about any kind of *just human action* until the human is *made just*. Consequently, if the doctrine of sin is the tendency toward self-realization by furious activity, then human agency must be excluded from assisting in the justification of the sinner.

Sin is, for Jüngel, secondly, the drive toward relationlessness as such. In his early book *Death: the Riddle and the Mystery*, Jüngel identified relationlessness with death.[19] What we fear most about dying is that it deprives us (we think) of the chance to have meaningful relationships with our loved ones, with ourselves, and most acutely, with God. Consistent with his conception of sin as self-fulfillment, Jüngel says that we try to actualize ourselves, to become our own lord, and this has the effect of cutting us off from our life-giving relationships. Instead, as he writes in *Death*, "Not to be one's own master does not imply some anthropological lack. It is rather an indication that man can live only in relationships, that since he stands at a distance from himself, he cannot be related to himself without at the same time standing in a relationship with God."[20] We cut ourselves off from these relationships at our peril. Lost in all the activity of self-fulfillment is the recognition that God has already acted in us, that at every moment God is relating to us and fulfilling us. Any actions that we perform should be viewed not as fulfillment per se, but rather as the natural response to a prevenient, fulfilling grace which allows for our action.[21]

Every day, people seek meaning and fulfillment in activities like marriage, employment, child rearing, physical pleasure and recreation, community service, education, and myriad other forms of the *vita activa*. Even if by our activity we seek to establish relationships with others, we are sinning, in a certain sense. After all, I may look at the relationship into which I have entered and see my own work in its creation, not God's. I cannot recognize relationships with others and with God as the gift they are if I think I constructed them. The relationships formed in all that activity are well and good, Jüngel wants to say, but the concomitant danger is that those relationships can so easily become distorted and dissolved. And this is sin. In Jüngel's own words, "In the Old Testament, man's life is determined by his relationships laid down in the law: relationships to one's neighbor, to the nation, to oneself, and to God. Men may seek to obscure and dissolve the simplicity of these relationships. The attempt to do so is what the Old Testament calls sin."[22] Any kind of activity by the human in the event of the justification of the sinner therefore risks distorting justification into the very thing it seeks to overcome: sin itself.

The third conception of sin relevant for Jüngel is unbelief. Since Jüngel mostly capitulates to Luther's formulations, I will be very brief in this area. In his most extensive work on the doctrine of justification, Jüngel writes, "In our unbelief we have withdrawn from God. We want to be something all by ourselves. That is why we refuse to allow God to be there for us. We want to exist—to stand out by ourselves."[23] Instead, we should realize that we owe a debt of gratitude to God. When we do not acknowledge this debt, Jüngel uses the metaphor of becoming mute.[24] As sinners turned in on ourselves in unbelief, "We lose our ability to speak our faith . . . Of course, we can hide our speechlessness behind vapid chattering, but the fact remains that we have nothing to say about God. By refusing to utter the one thing we have to say as sinners, our confession of sin, we have nothing at all to say before God."[25] What action of ours could we possibly speak of that might contribute to, even cooperate with, the God who speaks and justifies? Jüngel hints at the possible answer by asserting, "Such speechlessness is the passive dimension of that active urge to relationlessness of which we spoke."[26] Recognizing the passivity inherent in the human person's inability to believe in God, inability to relate rightly to God, self, and others, inability to actualize and justify oneself—this incredibly nuanced vision of human passivity—is one contribution Jüngel makes to theological anthropology, and its deformation in human tendencies toward isolation and relationlessness is a bracing insight into one way of describing human sin.[27]

ACTING UP: SIN AS REBELLION

Our third sin synonym evokes not just the intraself tension of estrangement and rebellion, but makes God a more central figure in understanding sin. This is sin as rebellion. To rebel sometimes carries heroic connotations, such as the rebellion of slaves against their wicked masters and in search of freedom. It can also bear a kind of childish connotation, as in the needful stage of young people rebelling against their parents or some other authority that marks the passage into and from adolescence and adulthood.[28] We saw in Chapter 2 that the OT in particular makes usage of rebellion as a metaphor for sin. The law of God was known, and accepted as legitimate, by many characters in Israel's story who nonetheless flagrantly and willfully contradicted Torah.

Illustrative exegesis: Romans 5.14–17

We turn once again to Paul for insight into the opposition to God inherent in understanding sin as rebellion. Specifically we turn to Paul's masterwork, Romans, the middle sections of which contain his longest and most nuanced uses of the notion of sin. After asserting (not arguing) that all have sinned, and thus all stand in need of grace, in preceding chapters, he begins anew with a Christological emphasis, namely that the obedience and righteousness of Jesus Christ opens a way for sinful humanity to reconnect in fellowship with God. Here is the passage in question:

> Death exercised dominion from Adam to Moses, even over those whose sins were not like the transgression of Adam, who is a type of the one who was to come. But the free gift is not like the trespass. For if the many died through the one man's trespass, much more surely have the grace of God and the free gift in the grace of the one man, Jesus Christ, abounded for the many. And the free gift is not like the effect of the one man's sin. For the judgment following one trespass brought condemnation, but the free gift following many trespasses brings justification. If, because of the one man's trespass, death exercised dominion through that one, much more surely will those who receive the abundance of grace and the free gift of righteousness exercise dominion in life through the one man, Jesus Christ.[29]

Adam's sin was rebellion. It was a "trespass" in the sense of a person who knowingly crosses a border across which one ought not to go.[30] In doing so, Adam's sin was like those of many who came after him, but even those whose sin did not exactly mirror Adam's own are still under the "reign of death" in sin.[31] Adam and his sin thus constitute a "type." The word "type" means something like "pattern setter." When a mold is made at a factory, every product that comes from the mold bears its particular shape. Adam rebelled against the life-giving command of God, and thus the "type" or "mold" of humankind was deeply harmed. The words used for Adam's sin in this passage are *paraptoma* and *parabasis*, both of which imply a kind of willful, intentional contradiction of an explicit command of God. And Adam's actions are a kind of representative, or typological, action for all those who follow him. Fortunately, a new mold has been cast by the "type" of Jesus Christ. The righteous obedience of Christ inaugurates a new type in a way that is much more powerful than the willful, type-changing rebellion of Adam.

We saw in Chapter 2 that for Paul, sin can take on a life and a power of its own. Something like this happens in Romans 5–8 generally, and in this passage particularly. It is not enough for a human to veer away (perhaps even unintentionally) from her or his intended target. Sometimes the power of sin is so strong that the sinner willfully flaunts wickedness in the face of goodness, craving the rebellion it brings with it. Even though the "judgment following one trespass brought condemnation," Paul does not leave us with the thought that the one who undergoes such judgment is particularly remorseful about it. But the one who is fortunate enough to have the rebellious motivator of sin be replaced by the obedient motivator of Christ can experience the joy of corresponding moral renewal. Thus we see a sense in which Christlikeness is precisely the obverse of sin, and in such an examination of Christ, the nature of sin becomes much more readily apparent. Precisely this strategy is put to use by a particularly faithful son of Paul's thought in the past century, Karl Barth.

Exemplary modern thinker: Karl Barth

The Swiss Reformed theologian Karl Barth (1884–1968) claimed that to attempt a freestanding "doctrine of sin" was not possible. Since sin did not have an ontological status, it could not, and should not, be directly described. Rather, sin is a kind of shadowy thing which, when light is cast upon it, is not illumined, but rather chased away. When seen in the light of the grace of God revealed in Jesus Christ, sin is not illuminated, it is destroyed. This approach makes sin a particularly difficult to understand element in the writings of the twentieth century's greatest religious thinker. But the seriousness with which Barth took sin, as well as the energy Barth devoted to coming at sin from a variety of angles, as it were, warrant a closer look at his understanding of human nature and its corruption in sin. Calling his approach to sin "rebellion" admittedly flattens out some aspects of his hamartiology, but captures others with special keenness.[32]

Barth's position on human nature, action, and sin can appear, at first glance, to be a tautology. Human action is sinful when it contradicts human nature. That is, when we act contrary to our true being, which as a creature is to glorify God the creator, we sin. So in sinning, we actually do something foreign to ourselves. In a vein of thinking traceable back at least as far as Thomas Aquinas, Barth writes, for example, "God does not ask of man that he should be something different, but simply that he should be what he is."[33] As the brilliant Barth scholar Matthew Rose puts it, "To be who we are: this deceptively demanding phrase captures that which is most intimate and proper to us and also that which is furthest and most difficult. God calls us to become who we are in Jesus Christ and yet it is something we are incapable of doing on our own."[34] We cannot be who we are if we try to be *ours*. We sin when we rebel against this fundamental dependence, and end up becoming, in sin, what we are not. As celebrated Barth exegete George Hunsinger nicely summarizes, "We are called (and called again and again) to be and become who we are. We come to see that we are (and are to be) in him and for him and with him, just as he is (and is to be) with us and for us and in us."[35]

What, then, is this nature that we rebelliously contradict in sin? The most real, the most natural, and most essential feature of humanity is participating in the life of the triune God in grace. As Barth says, "There is no one . . . who does not participate in Him in this turning to God. There is no one who is not himself engaged in this turning. There is no one who is not raised and exalted with Him to true humanity."[36] While this is true, we do not always experience this truth. We nonetheless are moral agents "who have refused His salvation and in that way denied their own destiny and perverted and wasted and hopelessly compromised their own being, life and activity."[37] Looking about we see that "Man does not recognize grace. He does not want it. At bottom he hates it."[38] Even when aware of our true calling to quintessential humanity, as Barth writes his commentary on the book of Romans, "Everything human swims with the stream either with vehement protest or with easy accommodation."[39]

Sin has a kind of cognitive content, then. I mean this not so much in the sense that when sinning one gives (possibly good) reasons for bad actions, but in the sense that James Gustafson names as "misconstruing that realm of reality that engages us; it is a matter of the wrong depiction and interpretation of the particular 'world' that attracts our attention and evokes our activity."[40] Living well is living in conformity to one's created nature, and sin is its obverse; it is living in conformity to the "shadow side" of creation. It is acting in conflict with our "most proper being."[41] Barth's notion of sin is thus connected to his understanding of evil, which is located not in the distorted will of the sinner, but in a metaphysical construal of creation. God creates by positively "electing" that some possibilities become actual. In doing this, God lovingly brings into being all that he affirms. Yet this affirmation implies a kind of negation. The logic of God's "yes-saying" implies that there is something to which God says "no." God's creative activity, in Barth's way of seeing things, includes within it a simultaneous repudiation of that which is not God's creative intent. This is true of all of creation, but particularly so of humanity. God's eternal election of humanity in Christ is the affirmation of his will, and through this *logos*, he creates humankind. The name Barth gives to that which stands in opposition to this nature is *Nichtige*, or "nothingness." The one and only way in which this nothingness "is," is as the recipient of God's repudiation.[42] To sum up, Barth writes, "When in creation God pronounced His wise and omnipotent Yes He also pronounced His wise and omnipotent No. . . . He marked off the positive reality of the creature from that which He did not elect and will and therefore did not create. And to that which He denied He allotted the being of non-being, the existence of that which does not exist."[43] Evil is the active power of this nothingness. And sin is evil active in human hands.

To sin is, in the truest sense of the word, to do *nothing*. In sin we are connected to what God has shunned, and give being to that the existence of which God denounces and indeed destroys. To find being in that which God "creates" as nonbeing is, in a word, absurd. Barth thus refers to sin as the "impossible possibility."[44] Sin is thus not only "against" God—against God's honor, word, and law. Sin is also "against" human nature itself. In sin humans make "ourselves impossible before Him and in that way miss our destiny, tread under foot our dignity, forfeit our right, lose our salvation and hopelessly compromise our creaturely being."[45] Or as Barth writes elsewhere, "He sins against himself. When he wills and does that which is evil he makes himself a stranger to himself; he loses himself."[46]

While sin is therefore ridiculous, absurd, and in a carefully quali-
fied way "impossible," Barth thinks that truly sin is *rebellious*. Barth
asserts that, seen from the perspective of Christ, we are all "defiant
sinners, the obstinately godless, the open enemies of God."[47] Building again on his conviction that sin cannot be seen by its own light,
but only in the light of Christ, Barth thunders, "the man of sin, his
existence and nature, his why and whence and whither, are all set
before us in Jesus Christ, are all spoken to us directly and incontro-
vertibly: Thou art the man! This is what thou does! This is what thou
art! This is the result! We hear Him and we hear this verdict. We see
Him, and in this mirror we see ourselves, ourselves as those who
commit sin and are sinners. We are here inescapably accused and
irrevocably condemned . . . Knowledge of sin at this point consists in
the knowledge: I am this man."[48]

The foregoing has operated at the level of conceptual orientation.
To say that Barth's doctrine of sin is an account of human rebellion
is to say that, in general, sinful humanity contradicts the nature
God has graciously offered it. In general, sin is irrational—even
"impossible"—because its grounding is in a surd. But what does this
mean, concretely? If showing a video clip of a human "sinning,"
what would Barth point out? How do we deny ourselves, miss our
goal, and ignore our call? Barth's explanation of sin in the concrete
relies on a construal of three notions, which together name sins as
such. They are: *pride*, *sloth*, and *falsehood*.[49] As Matthew Rose ele-
gantly notes, in pride, sloth, and falsehood, "We ascribe to ourselves
a dignity which we lack, deny ourselves a dignity which we possess,
and lie to ourselves about the truth—we become, in short, superhu-
man, subhuman or inhuman."[50]

First, pride. Barth does not mean by "pride" any sort of superficial
psychological impression of oneself. Rather, Barth means something
like a fundamentally inordinate expectation of what one can do on
one's own, of what one has oneself to thank for. Since God the benefi-
cent creator gives grace and blessedness freely, built into the logic of
creation is the orientation of creature as "grateful." In fact, one could
say that for Barth, God "wills" gratitude from the creature. The nature
of pride is that not only do we not render such gratitude, but instead
ascribe our being and blessedness to ourselves. Sin, seen by these
lights, is pride, the refusal of gratitude, "the one but necessary thing
which is proper to and is required of him with whom God has graciously entered into covenant."[51] Since the true nature of humankind

is revealed in Christ, and since Christ's humanity consisted in his humbling before God in the symbol of Golgotha, pride can be understood as the negation of God's merciful act of humility. "It is the fall in the form of presumption, acting as though God had not humbled Himself to man, as though He had not encountered man as the unfathomably merciful one . . . Sin is man's act of defiance."[52]

Second, there is sloth. If pride is aiming too high in our estimation of ourselves, of taking liberties that ought to belong to God, then sloth is pride's reverse. We sin in estimating ourselves too little. We resort to activities that only animals rightly ought to do. We assume that other humans are not worth our love and fellowship, and thus treat them sinfully. In Barth's words, "Sin has not merely the heroic form of pride but also, in complete antithesis yet profound correspondence, the quite unheroic and trivial form of sloth. In other words, it has the form, not only of evil action, but also of evil inaction; not only of the rash and arrogance which is forbidden and reprehensible, but also of the tardiness and failure which are equally forbidden and reprehensible."[53] The command of God to love one's neighbor demands attention to its content. The Christian life is not one of navel-gazing and complacency, but one of directed energies, mutual upbuilding, and striving after justice. What one might call a "sin of omission" is, then, sloth.[54] As Barth puts it, "If we consider sin only in its first and more impressive form it might easily acquire an unreal and fantastic quality in which we do not recognize the real man whose heart . . . is not merely desperate but despairing. . . . The sinner is not merely Prometheus or Lucifer. He is also . . . a lazy-bones, a sluggard, a good-for-nothing, a slow-coach and a loafer. He does not exist only in an exalted world of evil; he exists also in a very mean and petty world of evil."[55] The sinful person of sloth is one who is content with despair, satisfied with inaction, and imprisoned in mediocrity.

Seen in its first two forms, pride and sloth, sin thus leave the sinner unmoored, unhinged. Called, and offered the chance, to conform to her or his created nature, the sinner overextends or underperforms. The sinner "thus hastens forward without guidance or direction, abandoned to the control of this image, with neither plan nor goal nor limit, scurrying hither and thither, with no definite orientation, open on all sides, ready for anything, and therefore not really free, but the prisoner of his own empty demand for extension, and therefore of his inner caprice and external fate."[56]

Thus we come to sin in its third form, falsehood.[57] Falsehood is a "knowing better" than God how human life is to be lived.[58] It is "self-destruction; because man and the world live under the dominion of sin, lying to God and deceiving themselves, they live in self-destruction. At this point it is plain that sin cannot say Yes but only No, that it cannot build up but only pull down, that it can create only suffering and death. Sinful man is as such man without hope." Sin as falsehood is not the same as instances of lying. Falsehood is the root of lying (and other sins). To engage in falsehood is to try to suppress the inexorable power of truth to liberate. And as Barth understands truth to be a trait of personhood (particularly Christ's personhood) rather than a characteristic of statements, so too is its opposite, falsehood, also primarily to be predicated of *persons*. A sinful human *is false*. "As the effective promise of God encounters man in the power of the resurrection of Jesus Christ, man proves himself to be a liar in whose thinking, speech and conduct his liberation by and for the free God transforms itself into an attempt to claim God by and for himself as the man who is bound in his self-assertion—a perversion in which he can only destroy himself and perish."[59] Sin as falsehood implies an attempt to avoid an encounter with the truth of the word of God. Falsehood is not so much lying as it is evasion, and as such is especially sin in its "very earnest, respectable, devout and Christian form."[60] By way of concluding, consider the following passage, in which Barth describes how easily Christian faith can substitute sinful falsehood for pure truth:

> This is how falsehood speaks. This is the view of the man of sin. He does not question the truth. He does not oppose to it any antithesis. He does not persecute it. Nor does he ignore it . . . In his real enterprise he kisses his Master as Judas did in Gethsemane. He is not against the truth, but with it and for it, appealing to it with sincerity and profundity and enthusiasm, constituting himself its diligent pupil and strict teacher, making it his business to defend and propagate and magnify it. . . . Surely, it is a masterly way of escape when man succeeds, or thinks he succeeds, in handling the truth by facing it as he must, and yet at the same time avoiding it, namely, by changing or transposing it into a translation of his own, into an improved edition, in which it looks most deceptively like itself. . . . In his prime the liar confesses the truth with the greatest emphasis and solemnity. He accepts the truth of

God, the truth of man, Christian truth. The only thing is that it has become untruth, since in his mouth it can only be the truth which is taken in hand and inspired and directed by him . . . The only thing is that its thrust is now intercepted and its impact blunted. The only thing is that it is now directed into exactly the opposite of its original direction.[61]

As the foregoing has shown, according to Barth, when sinning "Man does actually will the impossible . . . He sets himself in mortal self-contradiction."[62] In systematically opposing our created nature we show "our persistence in the direction to that which is not. Man wills that which according to His incarnation God does not will. He wills the impossible. He wills to be a man without and even in opposition to his fellow-man. . . . He does not live a genuinely human, but an inhuman life, because he does not live as a fellow-man."[63] Separating these dimensions of sin into forms of pride, sloth, and falsehood, sin can also be unified as the sinner's denial of *oneself* in light of the truth of grace. Sin leads, then, to "false and inauthentic existence."[64] Sin is not just damaging. In fact, it is utterly devastating to the creature and its nature.[65] In the state and acts of sin, understood primarily as *rebellion* against one's true created nature, and thus against God, the sinner "wills himself in the disorder, discord and degeneration of his nature."[66]

ACTING OUT: SIN AS SELF-JUSTIFICATION AND SCAPEGOATING

A basic conviction that undergirds this whole book is that people more or less know the difference between right and wrong. That we do so seems obvious to me, actually. A full defense of this position would be impossible in a book like this, but for a brief insight into what I mean, consider the phenomenon of *lying*. When someone has done something wrong and is later confronted about it, many will immediately lie about what they have done. Besides further compounding our sin (and therefore, our troubles!), lying exposes the fact that when we seek to cover up what we have done wrong, we positively show our ability to tell right from wrong. When we lie about what we have done, we tell a story about the way things are (or, at least, about the way things seem to us). We place ourselves on the side of what is good and right and "true," and often, when necessary, place others on the side of what is bad and wrong and "false." This fundamental dishonesty with oneself and with others is a dimension of sin.[67] To be human is to "emplot" oneself in a story. To be a *sinful* human is, in a sense, to tell the story wrong.[68]

An example will help show what I mean. I know a person who was recently fired by his employer for "moonlighting"—working a second job in a way that negatively affected his job performance at his primary employment. He could not deny that his work was suffering. He was often late, often called in "sick," and was often too tired to be fully present with his duties. When confronted by the employer about this, the person immediately began to "contextualize" or "emplot" these details into a narrative that sought to make sense of them in a different way than the employer did. The employer strung together the evidence in a way that made the employee out to be the bad guy, in a way that justified the firing. But when the employee defended himself, he noted things like, "My mother has been ill, and did not have health insurance. I needed the extra money to pay her bills." "I couldn't stand my co-workers here—I needed to find some other people to spend time with." When it became clear that this defense wasn't working, he contextualized the confrontation in a different way. "You've always had it out for me since I came here—you never supported me the way I deserved to be supported."

The facts of the matter were not disputed. What was disputed was *how to make sense of them*. We make sense of our experience by contextualizing, or emplotting, them into a wider narrative. The way we tell the self-implying narrative of our actions can be every bit as sinful, and dishonest, as the sins themselves.[69] Our fallen human nature tempts us always to excuse ourselves, which often has the side effect of blaming someone else—making a scapegoat.

Illustrative exegesis: Genesis 3.11–13

We examined in considerable detail the Garden of Eden story in our chapter on original sin. But some dimensions of that story have not been fully clarified. When read from the perspective of sin as self-justification, the story comes alive in our minds. We see that the problem with Adam's and Eve's actions was not just that they contradicted God's law, or brought about certain ill effects, but rather includes their fundamental dishonesty in denying responsibility for what they had done. The text reads,

[The Lord God] said, "Who told you that you were naked? Have
you eaten from the tree of which I commanded you not to eat?"
The man said, "The woman whom you gave to be with me, she
gave me fruit from the tree, and I ate." Then the Lord God said to
the woman, "What is this that you have done?" The woman said,
"The serpent tricked me, and I ate."[70]

Here sin and blame begin a great domino effect. Adam sins, and
when confronted, blames Eve. In doing so, he secretly implies that
God bears some blame, too ("the woman whom *you gave me* . . .).
When Eve is confronted, she blames the serpent. In some rabbinical
texts, the serpent is confronted by God, and the serpent blames God.
"After all, *You're the one who made me* . . . "[71] In a word, such blame
passing is simply a lie. The sinner wants to locate the cause of sin in
someone or something else. Commenting on this passage, Luther,
with his characteristic attentiveness to the subtleties and subterfuges
of sin, remarks, "Finally the sinful person would rather accuse God
than acknowledge his own sin. Adam should have said, 'Lord, I have
sinned.' But he did not do this. He accuses God of sin and in reality
says, 'Thou, Lord, hast sinned. For I would have remained holy in
Paradise after eating of the fruit if thou hadst remained quiet."[72]

On similar grounds, Jesus consistently criticized the Pharisees of
his day, even though they, like he, had a high regard for the law, or
Torah, believed in the resurrection of the dead, and shared a resistance to empire. For example, Jesus says, "Beware of the yeast of the
Pharisees, which is hypocrisy." Or again, "Woe to you, scribes and
Pharisees, hypocrites! For you are like whitewashed tombs, which on
the outside look beautiful, but inside they are full of the bones of the
dead and of all kinds of filth" (Mt. 23.27). Jesus does not find blame
in the Pharisees for their diligent moral striving, nor in their high
regard for the law and its virtuous works. Instead, as Ted Peters has
noted, "They were assuming that if they could orient their lives to
God's will, then God would approve and favor them. In concentrating on this task of conformity to their perception of the divine will,
they had become blind to their own contribution to the aggression in
the world about them." Since they contextualize their actions so
myopically, "Whereas they thought themselves to be just, their attitude in fact spawned injustice. Whereas they thought themselves to
be loyal to the teachings of the prophets, they belonged in the league
with those who murdered the prophets." (Mt. 23.31–2).[73]

Exemplary modern thinker: René Girard

One utterly fascinating modern thinker who has helped us to see the roots of sin and evil in the desire of humans to self-justify their actions by scapegoating others is the French philosopher and anthropologist René Girard. The centerpiece of his analysis of violence is what he calls the "scapegoat mechanism." The word scapegoat itself comes from William Tyndale, whose 1531 translation of the Bible into English rendered Leviticus 16's "Azazel" as "scapegoat," meaning the "goat that escapes" or departs.[74] The ancient Hebrew ritual at Yom Kippur, described in Leviticus, involved the high priest symbolically placing the sins of the people onto one goat, which was then released into the wilderness, and the same high priest would sacrifice another goat to God. The purpose of this ritual is to purify the community of its sins and violence by placing them all onto these animals, which were then removed from the community, sins and all. Girard has written extensively about this ancient Jewish practice, identifying it as only one particularly vivid instance of a nearly universal phenomenon. For Girard, the scapegoat mechanism is the origin and sustenance of society, and provides insight into the dark recesses of human nature. Humans are prone to violence, and when such violence threatens to destroy social relationships, a way of diverting that violence is needed. Girard's scapegoat theory is complex and highly nuanced. However, three features are salient for our purposes here: *scarcity*, *desire*, and *violence*.

We live in a world where resources are scarce. This is the basic premise of such disparate fields as economics, politics, and evolutionary biology. What goods there are, from food to clothes to money to rights and responsibilities, are fundamentally finite. While there may be enough goods for everybody to have some of them, there are normally not enough for everyone to have all that they desire. We humans have a nearly insatiable appetite for the objects of our desire; we want more of what we already have, and we wish to sample that which we do not have. Yet greed and scarcity are utterly at odds. This creates competition and struggle.

Numerous critical observers look to greed and scarcity to explain human violence. Appeals to Darwinian accounts of scarcity, struggle, and "survival of the fittest" are prominent examples. However, Girard finds arguments from material scarcity to be insufficient. He points out that we do not just desire scarce goods as such, and for their own sakes. We also desire other subjects, as in the ancient conception of *eros*, and we also may desire that other subjects would desire us, as Hegel and others have pointed out.[75] But most of all, Girard says, we desire *according* to another. That is, our conception of what is good and what is therefore desirable is largely determined by the desires *of* others. We see what they want, we see what they have, and our desires are conformed to theirs. The conception of the good is communal, not individual, and the shared view of the good is passed along.

Girard therefore links violence to the desire of a scarce communal good. "The principle source of violence between human beings is mimetic rivalry, the rivalry resulting from imitation of a model who becomes a rival or of a rival who becomes a model."[76] The violence will persist and intensify because, as Girard notes, "In imitating my rival's desire I give him the impression that he has good reasons to desire what he desires, to possess what he possesses, and so the intensity of his desire keeps increasing."[77] Violence erupts between the rivals, and this violence must be dealt with. One rival could kill another, of course. That dynamic is common enough, as is illustrated amply by Girard's tireless philological work. But since no one is excepted from the risks of mimetic desire, this solution of the problem of mimetic rivalry can only end in the "war of all against all," of which Hobbes saw the awful secret.[78]

Instead of one rival killing the other, which when multiplied across an entire society would lead to utter chaos, the rivals tend to unite with each other against a common "enemy." "Suddenly the opposition of everyone against everyone else is replaced by the opposition of all against one. Where previously there had been a chaotic ensemble of particular conflicts, there is now the simplicity of a single conflict: the entire community on one side, and the on the other, the victim."[79] A society on the cusp of exploding into violence itself will try to alleviate the impending disaster by focusing its rage on just one component of the society. In Girard's writings, the scapegoat mechanism is usually treated at the level of the individual's dynamics of willing, consciousness, and action. He has sometimes resisted translating these (relatively) individualistic dynamics of the scapegoat mechanism into nonindividualistic terms. His hesitancy is understandable, as it is far from clear in what sense a group, such as a society or institution, may be said to "will" or "act." It seems at least plausible that a social group could be described according to the same conceptual scheme as is applied to individuals.[80] Yet either way, individually or corporately, the interrelation of desire, scarcity, and violence is plain.

Sin thus emerges in Girard's writings as a kind of pervasive side effect of the inability of humans to cope with scarcity and the anxiety it causes. But it is also a cause of evil, not just an effect, because each of our desires, and therefore our actions, are shaped by the desires and actions of others. Since those actions and desires themselves are tinged with the stain of sin, so will be all other actions which use them as a model. Even though each of us knows the difference between right and wrong, when we seek to self-justify our sinful actions by scapegoating another—in short, by aligning ourselves with what is good and others with what is bad—we delude ourselves and blur the difference between right and wrong. In the end, this is precisely *sin*.

I NEVER METAPHOR I DIDN'T LIKE: ON THE NEED FOR MANY SIN-NONYMS[81]

Religious concepts like sin, salvation, and even "God" are inexhaustible. No matter how richly one speaks of the reality toward which they point, it is never enough. We have seen this on our tour of some commonly used metaphors for sin in modern thought. We saw how estrangement, for example, captures the distance between human life as we can imagine it and human life as we live it, but left unexplained *how* the move from the ideal to the actual comes about. Speaking of relationlessness or isolation captures a slightly different element of sin, in that the process of estrangement leads inexorably to a cutting off of the relationships that constitute the essential self, or at least allow it to flourish. But the notion of isolation perhaps underappreciates the nefarious, quintessentially *active*, wicked dimensions to sin. The notion of "rebellion" captures the enmity with God that speaking of sin seeks to convey, by showing that our wrong actions are never ours alone, since we are not free to control the displeasure with which God sees them. But it cannot convey the kinds of minor, banal, unintentional sins that are the stuff of the everyday moral life. Must we decide between one conceptual scheme and another? If so, how might we do this?

To come at this question, let us briefly turn to a very helpful body of work in linguistic philosophy. George Lakoff and Mark Johnson, in their seminal work *Metaphors We Live By*, explore the way in which a kind of "master metaphor" for seeing a complicated, abstract, conceptual phenomenon can supply a range of smaller, concrete images that help to show the features of the more complicated whole.[82] Think of the master metaphor "time is money," for example. This gives rise to such expressions as "don't waste my time," "I've invested a lot of time in her," and "is that worth your while?"[83] What is important in seeing this pattern, however, is to keep constantly in mind that metaphors require both similarity and difference in the things being metaphorically compared. When you collapse the distinctions, the language becomes less effective. The person is best able to understand and communicate something about "time" when keeping in mind that, yes, time is *like* a valuable commodity, but that is not the only viable metaphor elucidating difficult notions of time. To switch the metaphor for a moment, think of the "master metaphor" that implies that an argument is like a war. This master metaphor gives rise to statements like "he attacked my position," "I had to defend my views," and so on. While this bellicose metaphor does help us to understand some things about argument, it also obscures others. For example, it might close our minds off to the ways in which argument can be collaborative and mutually upbuilding, oriented toward shared gains and problem solving, rather than just winning or losing.

When applied to the notion of sin, we see that this invites a kind of openness to a multiplicity of master metaphors for that inherently hard-to-pin-down notion. The logic of "relationlessness" might not be easily translatable into the language of "self-justification." But that does not mean that we must necessarily *choose* one metaphorical system to be "right" and another wrong. By maintaining a variety of conceptual schemes and holding them in tension with one another, we become uniquely able to see, in relief and in detail, features of sin that might otherwise be obscured. On this logic, the more "sin-nonyms," the better.

CHAPTER 5

SOCIAL SIN 1: RELATIONALITY AND THE FORMATION OF THE SINFUL SELF

Whether, in fact we regard [sin] as guilt and deed or rather as a spirit and a state, it is in either case common to all; not something that pertains severally to each individual and exists in relation to him by himself, but in each the work of all, and in all the work of each; and only in this corporate character, indeed, can it be properly and fully understood.

—Friedrich Schleiermacher, Christian Faith

Who am I? They mock me, these lonely questions of mine.

Whoever I am, Thou knowest, O God, I am Thine!
—Dietrich Bonhoeffer, Letters and Papers from Prison[1]

For a long, long time in Christian theology and theological anthropology, it was possible, indeed common, to conceive of sin wholly and exclusively in terms of the individual sinner. Sin was thought to be a distortion of the sinner's will, intellect, or reason. For Augustine, the root sin was pride. For Luther, it was unbelief. For Calvin, it was disobedience. But this kind of narrowness in approaching the doctrine of sin has been greatly questioned in recent years. In fact, at least two striking developments in theological anthropology have become practically axiomatic over the course of the last few decades. The first of these is that the doctrine of sin must no longer be understood solely in individualistic categories. The sins of which Christians in the latter half of the twentieth century were most keenly aware include, but are not limited to, such things as racism, sexism, the enforcement of global poverty, and the destruction of our natural environment. Such complex phenomena simply are not easily reducible to the discrete

sins of morally culpable individual agents. The evil is too complicated and too firmly located in social structures of human action for
us to think of the sin as being solely a matter of individual humans'
wills. The cumulative evil of the Holocaust cannot be simply the
added individual sins of each hand that organized a round up of
Jewish refugees, steered a railroad car of prisoners, or stoked a fur-
nace in a crematorium. We have recovered a sense of structural sin;
one that includes, but also transcends, the individual and the personal. The second development is the emphasis on *relationality* in
conceiving of the human self. No longer can we understand human
persons apart from the relationships that affect, or as some would
have it, *constitute*, their selves.

The office of the Vatican primarily in charge of identifying sins and
overseeing their absolution is known as the Supreme Tribunal of the
Apostolic Penitentiary. An official from this office, the Monsignor
Gianfranco Girotti, recently offered a list of seven "new" deadly sins.
Girotti was interviewed by the newspaper *L'Osservatore Romano*, and
therein outlined new ways that humanity breaches its relationship
with God. Girotti noted, "While sin used to concern mostly the *individual*, today it has mainly a *social* resonance." The new seven deadly
sins are: "bioethical" violations like birth control, "morally dubious"
experiments like stem cell research, drug abuse, polluting the environment, contributing to the widening divide between rich and poor,
excessive wealth, and the creation of poverty.[2] Whether one is sympa-
thetic to the new list or not, the point is that it does seem to symbolize
a new way of conceiving the phenomenon of sin. If sin is thought to
be easily localizable in the distorted will of the sinner, it becomes quite
hard to see how this view can square with something as interpersonal
and systemic as "contributing to poverty," or "polluting the environment." Those are social evils, and relatively little attention has been
paid, theologically speaking, to their interpretation.

Chapters 5 and 6 seek to illuminate this hitherto relatively ignored
dimension of sin—its sociality. In this chapter I look first at critiques
of individualism in sin that come from those who seek to view the
self in more *relational* terms. When the self is viewed as having come
to be in the presence of other, sinful selves—when the notion of personhood is unthinkable in abstract, solitary confinement—the notion
of sin as corruption of the self will necessarily become more social
and less individualistic. The next chapter will take a different
approach to the "social" in sin by tracking accounts of sin that see it

as a kind of "structure of oppression" or a "state of potent wickedness." Since such diagnoses of individualism in sin, and elaboration of structural doctrines of sin as an antidote, have come from Latin American and feminist liberation theologians, in particular, that chapter will look in detail at several important thinkers in those schools of thought.

The present chapter, far from being an exhaustive look at proposals for "the relational self," is intended to begin a conversation. The theme of this conversation can be stated something like this. "What would conceiving of the self in more thoroughly relational terms mean for understanding sin and culpability?" Our conversation will be a dialogue between three thinkers who have, in recent decades, elaborated an understanding of the self-in-relation.

THE NEED FOR A TURN TO RELATIONALITY

One of the most influential exponents of American philosophy[3] and of postmodernity in general is Richard Rorty. Rorty's devastating critique of foundationalist epistemology, his articulation of the contingent nature of selfhood and experience, and his skillful development of the resources of pragmatism to address various philosophical problems have won him legions of admirers.[4] However, he can be so blunt in prosecuting the postmodern agenda, and he uses such stirring imagery to articulate its content, that he has created a host of enemies as well.[5] In a famous passage from his midcareer work *The Consequences of Pragmatism*, Rorty wonders aloud whether the self has any grounding whatsoever. Is the self simply a collection of relationships, historically and culturally contingent, and not accountable to anything outside of the self? Such a view entails, Rorty writes,

> that when the secret police come, when the torturers violate the innocent, there is *nothing* to be said to them of the form 'There is something outside of yourself which you are betraying. Though you embody the practices of a totalitarian society which will endure forever, there is something beyond those practices which condemns you.'[6]

Hard as it is to believe, Rorty thinks that this view is accurate. There is no universal standard of right and wrong, and there is no ground outside of the self upon which the self is grounded. He continues,

This hard saying brings out what ties Dewey and Foucault, James and Nietzsche, together—the sense that there is nothing deep down inside us except what we have put there ourselves, no criterion that we have not created in the course of creating a practice, no standard of rationality that is not an appeal to such a criterion, no rigorous argumentation that is not obedience to our own convictions.[7]

Needless to say, this version of selfhood and culpability challenges an extensive tradition of Christian understandings of what it means to be a person and what it means to be responsible for sin. The rest of this chapter looks at just the aspect of the postmodern conception of the self in terms of the turn to relationality. Briefly put, no more can the self be thought to exist by itself, without reference to a whole host of *relata* which are not the self. The self exists in and because of a network of relations, if it exists at all.

To clarify and model ways that relationality contributes to human selfhood, and prompts a reconsideration of what it means to conceive of such selves as "guilty of sin," we turn now to an examination of three contemporary thinkers who have written extensively about the relational self, Marjorie Suchocki, Knud Løgstrup, and Paul Ricoeur. Roughly coeval, these thinkers differ greatly both in emphasis and content. They belong to different philosophical schools (process, Husserlian phenomenology, and existentialist phenomenology, respectively), and different theological traditions (Methodist, Lutheran, and French Calvinist). I outline the basic contours of their versions of the relational self and evaluate their adequacy in addressing the three main desiderata of the postmodern relational self. These desiderata will function as criteria in the investigation, which concludes that Ricoeur offers the best way forward in reconciling the Christian traditions on selfhood and sin with the turn to relationality in postmodern anthropologies. The desiderata are: (1) Allow for relationality to contribute to selfhood in nonsuperficial ways, (2) Allow for determinate links between selfhood and morally evaluable action, and (3) Do not resort to a "faculty anthropology" to restore the perceived loss of culpability in the relational self.[8] These are the only available criteria, but they are a good start. All three thinkers in the present inquiry make valuable contributions toward a relational Christian theological anthropology, and none escapes critique. But to foreshadow my conclusions with a woefully imprecise but nonetheless suggestive "Goldilocks" allusion, Suchocki's self-in-process seems to be *too relational*, Løgstrup's self *not relational enough*, and Ricoeur's hermeneutical self *just relationally right*. None of the three thinkers is so brash as Rorty in pointing to the drastic implications of the relational self, but all three are working in a context where critiques like Rorty's are taken seriously, and sin as a social phenomenon must be rethought.

WHITEHEADIAN RELATIONALITY: MARJORIE SUCHOCKI

Marjorie Suchocki is an advocate and apostle of "process" philosophy and theology. First articulated by the philosopher and mathematician Alfred North Whitehead, this way of thinking puts relationality at the center not just of human selfhood, but indeed of all of cosmic reality.[9] Suchocki's thoughts on relationality can be seen through the heurism of three concentric circles. The outer circle is the most general, consisting of a generic application of Whiteheadian metaphysics to the question of the human person. The middle circle, slightly more constrained in scope, construes the relationality of the outermost circle in terms of what must be the case in human relationships such that sin can result from them. Finally, the innermost circle of her reflections on the matter outline certain forms of human relationships, the presence of which allows for full human personhood, and the absence or deformation of which constitute human sin.[10]

We begin with the widest ring. At the most basic level, Suchocki says, we cannot describe who or what we are without reference to something else outside of ourselves. When asked about one's identity, for example, a common first response is to name a place of origin, which somehow contributes to whom the self thinks she or he is. One might also point to an occupation, or one could name a family connection. The point is, at the most basic level, personal identity cannot be described without naming the person in relation to virtually everything outside the person, and the sum of those relationships determines, in part, who the person is.

Those familiar with process philosophy in general will recognize this as the pattern Whitehead follows in his metaphysics. The most basic metaphysical concept is, for Whitehead, the *actual occasion*. An actual occasion is a transient, fleeting entity, always in the process of becoming. Suchocki summarizes Whitehead on actual occasions by describing them as "a drop of experience that comes into existence through the creative process of concrescence. They are the building blocks that, through an essential interconnectedness, make up the composite world of rocks, trees, and people."[11] The process of becoming weaves together what Whitehead calls "prehensions," which are something like feelings, or states of being related to, but often lack the conscious awareness that one actual occasion is prehending another. These elements "feel" each other, relate to each other spatially, causally, interactively, and so on. Each interaction between actual occasions is an event, and from that event a new actual occasion occurs. In Whitehead's memorable phrase, "The many become one, and are increased by one. In their natures, entities are disjunctively 'many' in process of passage into conjunctive unity."[12] Thence novelty arises, complexity increases, and "concrescence" occurs. Concrescence is the name given to this activity of becoming. It is the integration of various prehensions into an actual entity or actual occasion.[13] The process of the concrescence of prehensions into actual occasions continues indefinitely until such time as a "satisfaction" takes place. Satisfaction is said to occur when a subject's prehensions are integrated into a concrete unity.

In Whitehead's philosophy, which he called a "philosophy of organism,"[14] all of this is happening primarily at an incredibly small scale. Whitehead was, among other things, an expert in the emerging quantum theory, and many of his philosophical insights were derived from his observations of reality at the subatomic level. For Suchocki's anthropology, however, this all takes place at the macro-level. When a person is born, she can be described as an "actual occasion" who immediately has prehensions of the world around her. As those prehensions are synthesized in the process of concrescence, a new "actual occasion" emerges, though it is named by those in the outside world as the selfsame actual occasion all along.[15] As more and more prehensions become synthesized in the person, subjectivity emerges from the relational world. In contrast to idealist philosophers like Kant, for whom the already extant subject (especially her mind) "produces" the world around her, Whitehead and Suchocki conceive of the world as "producing" the subject by means of these processes.

This, then, is the broadest circle of relationality germane to Suchocki's anthropology. The second circle, included and implied in the first, but slightly more specific and constrained in scope, is the relationship of the self to time. The self, says Suchocki, is related intimately to her past, future, and present, and it is from a complex of these relations that sin is said to emerge. Suchocki writes, "The past, which was originally an objective reality into which one was thrown without one's consent, enters into one's subjective reality. When that past works against positive relationships that enrich the person, then that past is demonic."[16] The chances for the existence of nourishing interpersonal relationships are diminished by the facticity of their obscuration in the past. Obviously, this amounts to a version of original sin. While the past does not determine the future in Suchocki's anthropology, it does constrain what will be possible in the immediate future. "There is always a wedge of novelty [in the process model] that entails a degree of freedom and responsibility. The degree may be great or small, and the very reason for naming [the powers of the past] is because they leave but small room for freedom. But they cannot annihilate it completely."[17]

Another key aspect of one's relationship to the past comes in the form of the social institutions and structures which condition one's selfhood. In an extended analysis of Walter Rauschenbusch and Reinhold Niebuhr on the nature of unjust institutions, Suchocki points out that "individuals raised within such societies internalize the unjust norms, thus supporting them and ensuring their perpetuation. Since it is the individual *self*-consciousness that is so formed, it becomes constitutive of the self, and difficult to transcend . . . Original sin simply creates sinners."[18] The past builds a wall around us, separating us from life-giving relationships with God and others. "Sin imprisons one in a particular form of the past. By choosing to become a bearer of the demonic, one allows that past to become the determiner of one's reality."[19]

The temporally relational self is also intimately linked to the future. "There is also the imprisoning power of sin that comes, not from being overly bound by the past, but through fear of the future as death."[20] Borrowing a bit from existentialist philosophy, Suchocki notes that the fact of one's own impending death prompts a feeling of anxiety. "Knowledge [of one's death] brings the death of the future in to the present, annihilating the beauty of the present with the fear of that which is not yet."[21] The death of others to whom we are related breaks in upon us as well, since those relationships are internal to who we are, and so we cannot fully "survive" their deaths.

In the innermost ring, more focused still than Whiteheadian relationality and general temporality, are the three relations that constitute human personal identity, and the distortion of which constitutes human sin. These three relations are *memory*, *empathy*, and *imagination*. There is a kind of correlation between these three and temporality (memory with the past, empathy with the present, and imagination with the future), but each relation is more than just temporal. Suchocki thinks that the self can be described as existing in three phases. There is a "receptive phase" wherein the realities preceding the self converge, an "integrative phase" wherein the emerging subject creatively unifies those convergences, and a "projective phase" wherein the properly integrated subject joins the rest of the universe in the creation of ever more novel realities.[22] The self experiences the receptive phase in her memory. Past realities are called to mind. She thinks about the way things were, how she used to be, what she used to do.[23] But this is not enough, for rarely will old ways of being and acting perfectly map onto how the self should make sense of the present time. This requires empathy. By empathy she means not merely an emotion; rather this is the name Suchocki gives to the social character of the self. Empathy is the self's awareness of its surroundings and of the others in those surroundings. When the self acts in the world, it anticipates the consequences of its action by taking into account the reality of the other-than-self.[24] Finally, in imagination one transcends the present by envisioning a future not yet real, and by that vision one can participate in the transformation of the present.[25]

When these fundamental relations are obscured, sin results. The failure of memory causes the sin of the perpetuation of injustice. Selves (and groups, for that matter) who do not "remember well" do not grasp that the violence done in the past produced only pain and suffering. The self sometimes seems to stop at nothing to justify the perpetuation of such ways of being, however, by continually distorting memories and configuring them into a narrative of the legitimation of violence.[26] Empathy is prone to two distortions. When empathy is minimized, the self is absolutized, which is named by the sin of pride. When empathy is maximized, the other to which the self relates is absolutized, which is the sin of hiding or self-abnegation. Finally, a distorted imagination is sinful to the extent that it cannot envision a future which is different from the present, and cannot provide the self with an aim toward which she might exercise her freedom. All three of these relations—memory, empathy, and imagination— are forms of self-transcendence. Their distortion, sin, is violence.

Suchocki calls sin not rebellion against God, which is a kind of vertical description, but rather as violence against all creation, or as the perpetuation of ill-being.[27] God is, of course, affected by sin (in a process world, everything affects everything), but that is seen as a derivative of the primary manifestation of sin in distorted relationships. [28]

CRITIQUE

Where does the view of the relational self leave us in terms of our three criteria for evaluation? Clearly, Suchocki's version of the self does not fail to meet the first criterion, that of construing selfhood in nonsuperficially relational ways. In fact, just the opposite seems to be the case. By making the self contingent on a certain arrangement of certain relationships, Suchocki risks accounting for the presence of a self at all. A shortcoming of Suchocki's anthropology involves the status of the relational self as a moral agent. If, as Suchocki posits, the self is always "coming to be" or always "in process," at what point in the self's development has sufficient growth taken place such that one could say the self was now responsible for her actions, be they moral or immoral? Put another way, Suchocki's anthropology seems to have a *teleological* structure. Everything that is comes to be from the processes of concrescence and satisfaction, including the self, which means that the self only exists at the end of those processes. If that is the case, it seems that William Christian's criticism of Whitehead's metaphysics similarly applies to Suchocki's anthropology. In a particularly concise passage, Christian writes,

> If the structure of an actual occasion is teleological, and the realization of its aim is wholly extrinsic to the occasion, then we have a case of there always being jam tomorrow, never jam today. For suppose the satisfaction aimed at in the process A is realized *only* in the entities which succeed A, for example, B. Then the satisfaction of A will be a factor in the process of B. But this latter process aims at the satisfaction of B, which would in turn be realized only in C. Thus it would be true not only that the satisfaction of A is not realized in A, but also that there would be no finite entity in which the satisfaction of A is completely realized. It would follow that there is always becoming, but nothing becomes; there is creativity, but nothing is created; there are relations, but no genuine terms; there is causation, but no cause and no effect.[29]

Suchocki has a response to this sort of critique, but unfortunately in developing it she fails to meet the third criterion, for she emphasizes the necessity of the *faculty* of freedom when discussing moral culpability. Suchocki is forced into an argument for the presence of freedom in the moral agent without being able to offer an account of its origins or features. In discussing the power of the past to affect human choice in the present, I quoted above Suchocki's claim that "The power is greater than the individual, since it comes with the weight of a past that cannot be avoided. But in the process model there is always a wedge of novelty that entails a degree of freedom and responsibility. The degree may be great or small, but [the past] cannot annihilate it completely."[30] But where does this freedom come from? The simple fact that it is "entailed" by the logic of process metaphysics does not testify to its actuality. In a chapter on "Guilt and Freedom" in *The Fall to Violence*, it is as though Suchocki has to take back much of what she says about the relational self in the rest of the book, for she knows that it wars against personal responsibility. She says that it is only "given this freedom [that] there is an established basis for responsibility for one's actions."[31] But she surely has a peculiar version of this content. In what is usually the stock example of determinists, Suchocki compares the self to a rock.

> Even a rock is composed of electrons and atoms and molecules that in themselves have a response-ability relative to their past and to their environs. The rock changes, yielding to erosion and radioactive decay. The rock does not have freedom in a human sense, but in its very constitution, it has a response-ability that represents a miniscule indeterminism on a chain that includes, at its other end, what we call human freedom.[32]

But by "freedom" most people mean something more than "plasticity." For a human to be free is not to be theoretically manipulable by others. On the contrary, that seems to be the very definition of *bondage*. But I will not adjudicate that argument, since for our purposes here it suffices to point out that the logic of Suchocki's relational self eventuates in a situation in which individual responsibility is safeguarded by an appeal to a faculty anthropology. Such an appeal is a step backward in understanding the postmodern self.

HUSSERLIAN PHENOMENOLOGY AND THE SELF:
KNUD LØGSTRUP

Knud Ejler Løgstrup (1905–81) was a Danish philosopher and theologian who taught for most of his career at the University of Aarhus.
He is known primarily in Germany and America as an ethicist, since
his most widely read book, *The Ethical Demand*,[33] provides an elegant
application of his phenomenological commitments to the ethical
problem of neighbor love and personal responsibility. A compelling
case can be made to view Løgstrup as an ethicist, but he is also very
much a theologian and a philosopher. Little is at stake in defending
such distinctions, but I will note that many of the strengths and weak-
nesses of his ethical positions are rooted in anterior philosophical and
theological allegiances, so at least some of them need to be noted.[34]
Løgstrup was also known in his native Denmark as a powerful public
intellectual, where he attempted to rally responsible and effective
Christian opposition to Hitler's war efforts.[35]

Løgstrup studied philosophy early in life, describing an event at
age 16 when he abruptly stopped playing tin soldiers with a classmate
(who later became a Danish general!) and picked up Kant's *Critique
of Pure Reason*. His 1942 dissertation, which focused on neo-Kan-
tianism, was very critical of the tendencies of transcendental ideal-
ism to abstract too much from concrete instances of knowing in order
to show how such knowledge was possible a priori. His own philosophical preferences fell rather with phenomenology. Løgstrup was
very familiar with Husserl's thought, and maintained that Husserl
had gone very far in exposing the fraudulency of the dichotomous
subject/object schema that had characterized epistemology since
Descartes. However, in Løgstrup's eyes Husserl was still trapped in
the old ways of thinking. He could not see the unity of subject and
object in every instance of knowing to the degree to which that unity
was actual.

To ask "what is this self that exists in the world," we must not
abstract the self from the natural, concrete conditions in which it is
found. And that means that the self must be considered as a part of a
network of other selves. Each self is intimately connected with other
selves, and philosophy, Kantian versions thereof or otherwise, must
not commit the fallacy of misplaced concreteness by pretending to
abstract from that reality in focusing on the autonomous knowing
subject apart from its constitutive interpersonal relationships.

THE ETHICAL DEMAND

The starting point for Løgstrup's philosophy of selfhood and relationality is a phenomenological analysis of the central feature of all
interpersonal relations: trust. At the root of all of our dealings with
other people is trust. This trust is not always, or even usually, expressed
or articulated. But it is nearly always present. The fact that its absence
is so noticeable testifies to its near ubiquity. We do not need a reason
to trust others. We simply do, as a kind of default option. We normally do, on the other hand, need a reason to mistrust someone. We
also believe most people we encounter, unless we have good reason to
do otherwise. When the man behind the counter at the coffee shop
where I often read tells me that my coffee will cost $1.40, I simply
believe him and dig into my pocket. When a car salesman quotes me
a price on a used car, however, I may have reason to be suspicious,
since I have in the past known more shady car salesmen than coffee
shop owners. But the point is, our natural tendency is to trust and to
believe. This is true whether we want to trust and believe or not. Even
in so simple and fundamental an interpersonal phenomenon as a conversation, this trust is evident. Løgstrup writes,

> In the very act of addressing a person we make a certain demand
> of him. This demand is not merely for a response to what we say.
> What happens is that simply in addressing him, irrespective of the
> importance of the content of what we say, a certain note is struck
> through which we, as it were, step out of ourselves in order to exist
> in the speech relationship with him.[36]

It is out of this trust that the ethical demand emerges. Løgstrup
writes, "This trust means that in every encounter between human
beings there is an unarticulated demand, irrespective of the circumstances in which the encounter takes place and irrespective of the
nature of the encounter."[37] When we put our trust into another, we
are silently expecting certain things from them. If I trust that my coffee costs $1.40, and I pay the clerk that amount, I trust that he will
bring me my coffee. When I cross the street on a green light, I trust
that the woman in her car will obey her corresponding red light and
not run into me. My very participation in society implies that I am
trusting all sorts of different people and laws and customs at every
moment. And at every moment I am making a demand of them,

namely that they take me into consideration in their deliberations and actions. So central is this idea in Løgstrup's philosophy of the self that Lars-Olle Armgard writes, "According to Løgstrup, an eleventh commandment should be formulated today: Thou shalt not deprive any person of his or her personal responsibility for his or her own life and that of others."[38]

The demand is usually silent. It is simply the way of the world, not an enunciated strategy for living in the world. The obligations implied by the silent, radical, ethical demand are not easily formulated into permanent laws or rules that would be valid cross-culturally and for all time. Indeed, one of the most important features of Jesus's proclamation seems to be, for Løgstrup, its nonfocus on rules. Løgstrup states, in what could be considered a kind of summary of his project as a whole, "Since the demand is implied by the very fact that a person belongs to the world in which the other person has his [sic] life, and therefore holds something of that person's life in his hands, it is therefore a demand to take care of that person's life. But nothing is thereby said about *how* this caring is to be done."[39] The form that the reflective response to the demand takes is what is normally called ethics, and can presumably vary quite widely. Løgstrup's discussion of the demand is thus more descriptive than prescriptive. Løgstrup posits a distinction between the radicality of the silent demand and the mediated social norms in which the demand clothes itself. "The radical demand says that we are to care for the other person in a way that best serves his interest. It says that but nothing more . . . The social norms, on the other hand, give comparatively precise directives about what we shall do and what we shall refrain from doing."[40] Ideally, "the social norms serve as a guide in helping us to decide what will best serve the other person," but they may also lead us astray from their real need and our real responsibility.[41] The demand may not even be self-identical in intensity and exact shape across time and space. For example, a person who has been the victim of oppression or abuse may (justifiably) be so suspicious and untrusting of other people that distrust could begin to seem more basic to survival than trust. But if this condition does exist, it must be seen as an extreme diminishment in the life God intends for humans.

There are some similarities between Løgstrup's articulation of the demand and the golden rule. As Gene Outka notes, the golden rule instructs us to do unto others as we would have them do unto us, not to do unto others as they would have us do unto them.[42] So too, for

Løgstrup, we must not confuse how the neighbor would have us answer the ethical demand with how we ought to answer it. And in a corollary sense, we ought not evaluate our response overmuch on the basis of anticipated reciprocity. In fact, Løgstrup does not want any moral deliberations to depend on a calculation of what the person who has put themselves into your care will do for you. One's reaction need not be "spontaneous," but moral deliberation should not be reduced to means-end or cost-benefit analyses. The fact that the demand is "radical" means that it can be met only through unselfishness, or even more strongly, through love for all, even those who utterly forego their responsibility for us. In Løgstrup's view, even our enemies are utterly dependent upon us. Our unselfishness does not mean that we acquiesce to the stated requests of the person we face, however, any more than we should let the historically and culturally contingent social norms determine our response. We must deliberate on what would be best for the other person for his or her own sake, and do what is in our power to effect that.

SIN AND GUILT INFERRED

Sin could be defined in Løgstrup's thought as the refusal to respond appropriately to the ethical demand. This happens in two ways. The first, most obvious way in which we fail others (and therefore, according to Løgstrup and Gogarten, the way we fail God) is by not taking responsibility for the demand they make of us. We run roughshod over others in all manner of ways, great and small. We pollute, we steal, we lie. But the second way in which we breach the demand consists in not allowing others to care for us. We insulate ourselves from others. We refuse to interact with people who could enrich us, attend to us, and help us. In other words, part of sin as the violation of the ethical demand is a lack or distortion of proper interpersonal relationality.

There is a sense in which sin is thus inevitable. As in any network, a disruption in one region of a system of interrelated selves almost necessarily entails a disruption somewhere else in the system. The possibilities open to me to care for someone who has been entrusted to me are profoundly affected by the decisions previously made by others. Virtually no situation in which someone was entrusted to me could present the one unambiguously *right* response to their need. The fact that they are in need is likely the cause of a previous sin. When called on to adjudicate an argument among friends, for example, I find

myself unable to make all well. If I try to defuse their anger by focusing it somewhere else or making light of the situation, I risk not
addressing the problem. If I suggest they talk their anger through, I
risk unnecessarily opening old wounds. If I hastily recommend their
forgiveness of each other, I risk misplacing blame and creating bitter-
ness. I am not omniscient, and so therefore do not know the good well
enough to effect its unambiguous realization. I am not omnipotent,
and so therefore probably could not bring about the good even if I
knew what it was. Løgstrup puts this standard Augustinian distinction like this: the ethical demand is at once binding and yet unfulfillable.[43] This is a product of the inherent uncertainty in relating the
absoluteness of the ethical demand to the contingency of the social
customs in whose framework I must respond. Løgstrup summarizes,
pointing out the one tendency toward sin as excessive self-assertion.

The demand that I take care of the other person's life makes my
relation to the norms uncertain in the sense that it reveals how I arro-
gate the norm to myself as though I were its author. I insist upon this
norm, I exult over it, I use it for lording it over the other person, I
take vain pride in defending it. I remove all distance between the
norm and myself and thereby also remove the distance between the
other person and the norm.[44]

But this ambiguity can also lead to the other tendency of sin:
excessive self-abnegation. Driven to despondency by my inability to
do the greatest good, I may omit to do the relative good which lies
within my power of discernment and effort. To further the earlier
example, I may choose not to care for my arguing friends at all. I
could refuse to be the self that I could be. I may reject the possibilities
of interpersonal selfhood entirely, thereby shrinking away from the
very relationships that could be life-giving.

If the foregoing material on Løgstrup sounds familiar, it is probably because he and the great phenomenological philosopher Emmanuel Levinas have so much in common. Whatever the relationship
between the two men,[45] the close proximity of their respective philosophies warrants scrutiny, for many of the themes I have been trac-
ing through Løgstrup's thought appear in Levinas in slightly different
form. Levinas is perhaps more indebted to Husserl than was Løgstrup, even if sometimes more antagonistic towards his mentor. Even
when Levinas deviates from Husserlian phenomenology, he is careful
to develop his positions in contradistinction to Husserl's. Philosopher and sociologist Zygmunt Bauman links the two with a helpful

heurism. Whereas modern ethics had discussed "togetherness" in terms of "being-with," according to Bauman, Levinas and Løgstrup point the way forward into a postmodern ethic by transposing togetherness into "being-for."[46] Bauman notes,

> For Levinas, the beginning of morality is "the preoccupation towards the Other even up to sacrifice for him, even up to the possibility of dying for him." Awakening to the face—Levinas never tired of repeating—is tantamount to the shock of awakening to the inaudible call for assistance, which the vulnerability and weakness of the Other, revealed in the nakedness of the face, issues without speaking.[47]

Alasdair MacIntyre and Hans Fink delineate two helpful features of overlap between Levinas and Løgstrup.[48] First, for both thinkers, though perhaps especially so for Levinas, my responsibility for the Other whom I meet exists completely apart from the social context in which I meet her. It matters little whether I am rich, poor, old, young, American, French, or Danish. There is just something irreducibly *human* about being confronted by the face, not the mask, of another that implies something about what I must do, and how I must be responsible. Secondly, the content of my responsibility is not derivable from or even based upon *any* previous conception of ontological good. On the contrary, in a phrase often associated with Levinas, there is an "ontological primacy of the ethical."[49]

Another similar feature of Levinas and Løgstrup will lead us into the section on critiques of Løgstrup. While Levinas was a professional philosopher employed in a secular university for most of his writing career, he was also a commentator on the Talmud and was a devout Jew. While Løgstrup was a professional philosopher at a public institution, he was also an ordained Lutheran pastor and committed Christian. One might justifiably wonder whether each thinker is not smuggling in covertly theological concepts through the back door of a purportedly independent phenomenology of existence.

CRITIQUE

Two criticisms might be made of the way Løgstrup conceives of sin and the relational self. First there is the issue of whether Løgstrup commits the naturalistic fallacy, and second there is the question of whether (and if so, how) Løgstrup's phenomenological methodology causes him to bracket out forms of relationality *other than the ethical demand* which a thoroughly relational theological anthropology rightly ought to consider.

Does Løgstrup commit the naturalistic fallacy? That is, just because he has identified the fact that there *is* a demand, does that necessarily mean that there *ought to be* a demand? The naturalistic fallacy, first developed by David Hume, is a form of argument that tries to move from declarations of what is the case to injunctions of what should be the case. An example might be saying, "A close look at human history reveals the omnipresence of war. Every culture everywhere knew and knows war as a fundamental reality. Let us embrace this eternal truth and have our own war, aiming our missiles at North Korea."

Obviously, statements of obligation are often centered on facts. But they cannot be reduced to a statement of fact. The great British philosopher G. E. Moore uses the example of a gold ring. All the facts about the ring do partially contribute to a value judgment about the worth of the ring. It matters whether the ring is in good shape, whether it is truly made of gold, and so on. But taken by themselves, those facts will not tell you whether the ring is valuable. You must also know that gold rings are generally valuable. And the reasons for why that is true reside in a whole different set of analyses and facts. At some point, then, description of a state of affairs must give way to a judgment about the appropriateness of that state of affairs, and that judgment should be based both on facts and also on values.

What does this all mean for Løgstrup? Well, it does not necessarily mean that his argument is fatally flawed. He is open to this criticism, but not unavoidably wounded by it. It is true that he does base his entire work on the *fact* that selves put others in their trust and care all the time. It is also true that he argues from this "indicative" to the "imperative" that we should thus care for the others who trust us, and allow ourselves to be cared for by those in whom we put our trust. But we might very reasonably ask *why* this should be. Just because people do nearly always speed on California highways certainly does not mean that I should do so myself. Løgstrup anticipates this potentially devastating objection in a footnote:

> Someone will probably argue that the fact that a person gives himself to another person by trusting him is one thing, whereas the demand that we take care of the life thus committed to us through

trust is quite another thing; in other words, that there must be a difference between a fact and a demand, between an opinion about what is and an opinion about what ought to be. This argument raises a number of questions too extensive for treatment in this book; they must be dealt with elsewhere.[50]

It is true that value or "ought" judgments are intimately linked to facts about what is. When I tell my neighbor that he is using beams in the addition to his house he is building that are not strong enough, I am certainly blending *is*'s and *ought*'s. The beam *is* of a particular size, the addition *is* expected to support a particular weight and so on, but when I say that he *ought* to use larger ones, I am relying on rational deliberation, not phenomenological description. What Løgstrup does to insulate himself from this critique is to say simply that fact and demand are linked. He goes on to say, "Our concern here is only to point out the intimate connection between the fact and the demand, to point out that to a great extent the demand grows out of the fact. In other words, the fact forces upon us the alternative: either we take care of the other person's life or we ruin it."[51]

What Løgstrup should have done, and what would have been more effective, I think, is to say that in addition to the reality of the phenomenon of trust, there is the reality that our moral deliberations reveal values developed over time and through experience. This experience does not dictate my response to the need of my neighbor. The demand calls that forth. But I am, after all, part of a certain community at a certain place in time, and we have worked out some ways of being that have the weight of value judgments for coping with certain states of affairs. This probably implies being more up-front about theological commitments than Løgstrup has hitherto been; there is, after all, something distinctively Lutheran about pursuing ethics as radical faith active in radical love, and Løgstrup might as well admit that that is what he is doing. If Løgstrup had argued this way, he would have made himself less vulnerable to the critique of the naturalistic fallacy. Further, such argumentation would not force him in to such vagueness about the nature of the *authority* of the demand. He asserts, for example, that the authority of the demand rests in part on the fact that "the demand makes sense only on the presupposition that the person to whom the demand is addressed possesses nothing which he or she has not received as a gift."[52] It is not obvious that or how such a statement is true, philosophically speaking. Our lives are gifts from whom? Gifts of what? It seems more honest to forthrightly declare that his conception of selfhood rests on explicitly theological (Lutheran, no less) claims about God and grace. And the "ought" judgments we inevitably must make derive not just from the facts elucidated by impartial philosophy, but also from those theological commitments.

The second main critique is also based in methodology, but it is one from which I find it extremely difficult to vindicate Løgstrup. When phenomenology is done the way Løgstrup does it, the *causal history* of the subject must be bracketed out. That is, each event under scrutiny, usually a subject/object or subject/subject encounter, is examined in its particularity. Løgstrup and Lipps and Husserl ask, "What is happening in this event? What is the best description of this event we can offer?" And that means that you do not look at the encounters such a subject had in the past that brought her to this current event. You just look at the current event. The phenomenological approach of Løgstrup can expose, say, the parasitic reality of mistrust, or the all-too-real effects of such mistrust. It can even, as I showed above, offer vocabulary like "sin" to name this situation. But it cannot do what a theological anthropology must; such a phenomenology simply cannot account for *personal identity*. Persons are histories. Persons are stories. Persons always stand at the end of a long causal history and simultaneously at the beginning of a new one. Actions of the sort that Løgstrup analyzes simply must be intimately connected with their agents. And it is exactly that which Løgstrup's methodology disallows. There is no room in his analysis for looking at an instance of sin and saying, "Oh, I see that the person who did that was affected (or constituted) by his or her relationships in this or that way. I see that her mistrust was warranted or unwarranted. I see that her identity has taken this shape for these reasons" and so on.[53] The objection I am raising here is a criticism that stems from my first criterion, that we allow relationality to contribute to selfhood in non-superficial ways, as well as the second criterion, for there seems to be no room in Løgstrup's self for the self-identity so constituted to eventuate in morally evaluable action.

As opposed to conceiving of a self which is developed in its relations, Løgstrup's model is more like the following. There is a self. We do not know where it came from. We do not know much about what it is like. It probably has a history, and that history probably affects its actions and relationships with others. But it is this already constituted self which then relates. It is not created in its relations. While it may not continue to exist without those relations, it nonetheless appears to exist relatively independent of them. I think it is clear that offering anything less than the most intimate connection between relational agent and sinful action falls short of the challenge I have been posing throughout my project. A postmodern theological anthropology must come to terms with the simultaneous truths of personal identity constituted in relationships with that which is not the self, while not giving up on individual moral culpability. While Løgstrup helps us take important steps down the path to such a conception of the relational self, I think in the end he cannot take us far enough. We shall have to turn our attention to a different exponent of phenomenology, one who does not disallow a link between personal identity and morally evaluable action, and one with a more subtly conceived relationship between philosophical and theological anthropology. We turn now to such a figure, Paul Ricoeur.

EXISTENTIALIST PHENOMONOLGY AND NARRATIVE: PAUL RICOEUR

Writing about and reading Paul Ricoeur is a chore and a joy. It is a chore for two reasons. First, his philosophical works are astonishing in both their breadth and depth. Virtually no topic in philosophy, from ethics and political theory to hermeneutics and the meaning of history, has avoided Ricoeur's careful scrutiny. Though there is admirable consistency across fields in the positions Ricoeur takes, ferreting out the connections between topics on which he has written, especially on the question of selfhood, takes a lot of work. Secondly, like many great thinkers (Augustine, Barth, and Wittgenstein come to mind) Ricoeur has undergone a kind of conversion experience. His early work in existentialist phenomenology and the philosophy of the will was written before the so-called "hermeneutical turn" exemplified in his book *Freud and Philosophy*.[54] Readers of his work must therefore be judicious in comparing "early Ricoeur" with "late Ricoeur."[55] I attempt to avoid that pitfall by limiting my discussion of Ricoeur's work to the mature period after the hermeneutical turn, summarizing the representative work on selfhood from this phase, *Oneself as Another*.[56] I regret that the exposition of this masterful work shall have to be extremely compressed, simply taking the form of a summary. But this is necessary in order to leave room for an analysis and critique of the argument's adequacy in addressing our problem, as well as connecting up Ricoeur's work with Løgstrup's and Suchocki's.

As to the contested continuity of Ricoeur's early and late periods, I propose the image of a stone archway. One of the posts of the archway is his philosophy of the will and early existentialist writings. The bricks of which it is composed are taken from the structures built by Husserl, Marcel, and the early Heidegger. After writing *The Symbolism of Evil*, however, Ricoeur became convinced that he would have to suspend construction of this "post." No more would "description" alone suffice. He had to *interpret* the description. So he began building a second post, this one cobbled together with stones borrowed from Gadamer, literary critics, and the later Heidegger. He began to publish widely in all areas of hermeneutics, from literary criticism and biblical exegesis to action theory. This second "post" seemed on the face of it not to have much in common with the earlier philosophy of the will, save for the common ground upon which both stood. But the occasion to give the Gifford Lectures in 1986 prompted Ricoeur to connect these two structures. I consider *Oneself as Another* to be the lintel that arches between the twin posts of phenomenological selfhood and hermeneutics. For in this book he develops the concept of the hermeneutical self. The self is conceived along the lines of a text which is being written and interpreted and related to. It is my considered judgment that the resulting archway marks the best passage forward into postmodern conceptions of the relational self and moral culpability.

ONESELF AS ANOTHER

The French title of this book is *Soi-même comme un autre*, and three words in the title disclose the three main preoccupations of Ricoeur in the work. There is the question of the self (*soi*) as acting subject and the reflective meditation thereon, there is the sameness or self-identity (*même*) of that subject over time and space, and there is the dialectical interplay between that self and the other (*autre*) whom it meets. Ricoeur has always tried to remain critical of, yet appropriate from, Enlightenment philosophies of the self-positing subject. This he does again in *Oneself as Another*, positioning his own view of the self between the Cartesian *cogito* and the anti-*cogito* skepticism of

Marx, Freud, and Nietzsche. He asks, "To what extent can one say that the hermeneutics of the self developed here occupies a place situated beyond the alternative of the *cogito* and the anti-*cogito*?"[57] Situating the self takes the rest of the book, which is organized into four groups (in ten chapters). In doing so, Ricoeur asserts that he is trying to answer four main questions. The questions are: "Who is speaking? Who is acting? Who is telling his or her story? And who is the subject of moral imputation?"[58] My exposition of Ricoeur's work traces these questions through four groupings.

The first group comprises two chapters on the philosophy of language. Considering language as both semantics and pragmatics, Ricoeur undertakes a laborious detour trying to get clear on answers to the following questions: "How can I identify a person as a person?" "Or for that matter, how can I identify anything *as* anything?" "Are persons just bodies, numerically the same extended in time and space?" Ricoeur uses Strawson's philosophy to take the first steps toward a more concrete self, by accepting Strawson's thesis that all "individuals" are persons or physical objects.[59] In the second chapter, Ricoeur notes how humans are peculiar in the world in that they use language. The self comes to be, so to speak, not only in being named by identifying reference, but also in naming itself, or by utterance. This is a detour on the way to a study of selfhood, but it is a necessary one. If we are to have a hermeneutical self, Ricoeur thinks, we must take time out to analyze the language in which that interpretation shall take place. I should note that it is also an insufficient approach, for Ricoeur. Consider the following example. I can use the designator "Kirby Puckett" to identify the centerfielder for the Minnesota Twins from 1984 to 1995 who was a ten-time all-star, the 1989 batting champ, and the boyhood idol of a certain Derek Nelson. This is identifying reference, and it is very specific and helpful. There is only one person whom it identifies. However, this must be supplemented by the utterance of the subject. "Hi, I'm that Kirby Puckett" can be said by only one person. This, too, is a helpful step in getting at the selfhood of "Kirby Puckett," but it does not reconcile the first-person ontology of utterance and the third-person ontology of identifying reference. As we shall see, *narrative* must be added to these concepts.

The second grouping extends the philosophy of language to a philosophy of action. Answering "Who is speaking?" is, as Austin and Searle have shown, close to answering "Who is acting?" Here we see a distancing of the self from itself, as hermeneutics begins to show that the self is not transparent to itself, as it is in the *cogito* scheme. Comprising chapters three and four, this group of thoughts also assesses intentionality and causation. Noting Davidson's influential discussion of actions versus events, Ricoeur opts not to go very far down the path of analytic philosophy, but instead shows its short-comings. Basically, he writes, Davidson and Strawson and Anscombe and all the rest of the Anglo-American philosophers of action are only answering the "what" of action. *What* action is done? For *what* reason is it done? *What* person does this? And that is, of course, a question of *idem* identity, or exactly self-same identity, whereas Ricoeur is trying to articulate *ipse* identity, which is the identity of selfhood. This entails supplementing the above philosophy with a strictly hermeneutic philosophy, for in order to turn the *what* of an action into the *who* of an agent, we must know something about the agent's character, history, self-understanding, and so on. And those are questions of *interpretation*.

This passage is marked by the third grouping, comprising chapters five and six on "Personal Identity and Narrative Identity" and "The Self and Narrative Identity." Since this is really the turning point of the whole book, I will be a bit more thorough in my explication of this section. Finally, here, Ricoeur comes to his dialectic between identity as sameness and identity as selfhood. What Ricoeur is after is a "form of permanence in time that is a reply to the question, 'Who am I?'"[60] Ricoeur proposes two possible answers: the concepts of character and of promise keeping. Character means "the set of distinctive marks which permit the re-identification of a human individual as being the same."[61] This vaguely echoes Ricoeur's earlier work, like *Freedom and Nature*, where one's character was said to be a part of the involuntary in one's life, to which we perhaps consent, but scarcely change.[62] In *Fallible Man*, character was a boundary condition surrounding my potential openness to other persons, values, or ideas.[63] In *Oneself as Another*, however, it includes features like "numerical and qualitative identity, uninterrupted continuity, and permanence in time."[64] Character thus seems to be a part of idem identity. Promise keeping, on the other hand, entails not changelessness but constancy in the face of real change. When I promise something, "even if my desire were to change, even if I were to change my opinion or my inclination, 'I will hold firm.'"[65] This is ipse identity.

Narrative identity, the kind of personal self-understanding that Ricoeur is after, consists in the dialectical union of these opposing concepts. One could envision Ricoeur's self as an ellipse with two foci. The particular shape of the perimeter of the ellipse, which is the contour of selfhood, must be described in relation to the two points within the ellipse away from which it can never completely escape, the idem and the ipse. The faculties which are often said to compose human dignity, like reason, freedom, and consciousness, are part of the idem identity and must be respected as such. Contingent relations, like interpersonal relationships, social location, and destiny, are part of the ipse relationality. The successful self achieves the integration, though not the dissolution of the constitutive tension, by narrating identity in reference to these foci.

To explain how this is possible, we must take a brief detour to Ricoeur's narrative theory, especially as this is laid out in the work *Time and Narrative*.[66] There he proposes a threefold mimetic way of interpreting "narratively." First is mimesis$_1$, or *prefiguration*. Prefiguration, akin to Gadamer's idea of *Vorurteile*, involves the articulation of one's preconceptions in coming to a text. I may not know much about a certain text I am about to read, but I never come to it completely bias-less. For example, I recently read Hunter S. Thompson's *Fear and Loathing in Las Vegas*. I did not know much about the genre of "gonzo journalism" or what it is like to be that high on that much mescaline, but I do know something about the form of ordinary journalism, the style of William Faulkner, the general reputation of Las Vegas's decadence, and the fact that Thompson is basically insane. Such knowledge sets up the possibility of the interpretation of the text. The second stage is mimesis$_2$, or *configuration*. Drawing on these prefigurations and assumptions, configuration is both an author's construction of a text (by *emplotment*,) and a reader's imaginative construal of a text into their own imagination. Emplotment is the bringing together of events, agents, and objects into a meaningful whole. Events begin to be linked to causes, and a story begins to take shape. What this means for the self is that the contours of the narrative unity of idem and ipse selfhood emerge. I make sense of myself by telling my story. When I tell my story, I am both agent *and* patient, subject *and* object, narrator *and* character, self-same *and* relational, contingent *and* sovereign. Finally, in mimesis$_3$, or *refiguration*, we integrate the text into our experience. We apply what we have learned and become new. We are new because the self which came to the text with its prefigurations has been challenged and altered. This is both "undividedly revealing and transforming. Revealing in the sense that it brings features to light that were concealed and yet already sketched out at the heart of our experience, our praxis. Transforming, in the sense that a life examined in this way is a changed life, another life."[67]

This threefold mimetic arc of narrative interpretation is both a fundamental reality in nearly all textual interpretation as well as a skill to be learned and honed. It admits of a wide range of proficiency among its practitioners. Some emplot themselves nearly seamlessly in the story of their life, and some do not. As we shall see below, this fact has ethical implications, for one way of defining sin, evil, and the "fault" in humans is the characterization of an unethical narrative.

The final grouping of ideas in *Oneself as Another* (chapters seven, eight, and nine), after the philosophy of language, the philosophy of action, and the philosophy of narrative identity, is Ricoeur's mature ethics. This is also the point where the third word of the title comes into play, for here a final dialectic is added. The narrative self consists of the interplay between idem and ipse identity, but there is also the further dialectic of the self with the other. For it is in the encounter with the other that the ethical is determined. Ricoeur does not go so far as to say that the self is *produced* in the encounter with the other, but the encounter does play an important role, which is the role of *attestation*.

Ricoeur calls the concept of attestation the "password for this entire book."[68] Attestation is the kind of certainty that is appropriate to the postmodern self. It is neither the pure skepticism of Nietzsche nor the self-grounded certainty of Descartes. Rather, Aristotle's idea of practical wisdom seems to be the model, which is situated between objectivity and relativism. I am sure of my identity when my actions attest to my intentions, when my judgments attest to the evidence, and most importantly for our purposes, when the Other whom I meet attests to my identity. Ricoeur links attestation with Heidegger's notion of the conscience,[69] which calls forward authentic existence, as well as with Spinoza's language of *conatus*, of the desire to live well.[70] I think it is clear how much the logic of attestation is dependent on otherness. The notion of the self as the one who promises is of course dependent on having someone to make a promise to, as well as having someone who may attest to my constancy or unreliability.

Saying that the self is formed with a certain character assumes the otherness of those who shaped that character in the developing self, and who continue to attest to its endurance. Specifically in ethics, Ricoeur defines his own project under the slogan "aiming at the good life for and with others in just institutions."[71] Disputes about the subjugation of deontology to teleology notwithstanding, here, too, otherness is constitutive of the ethical self. I cannot undertake any ethical project without being "for and with the other" in a further social context (institutions). Another way of putting this might be to show the inherent "solicitude" implied in simply being human. In a stirring passage, Ricoeur writes,

> Solicitude adds the dimension of value, whereby each person is *irreplaceable* in our affection and in our esteem. It is in experiencing the irreparable loss of the loved other that we learn, through the transfer of the other onto ourselves, the irreplaceable character of our own life. It is first for the other that I am irreplaceable. In this sense, solicitude responds to the other's esteem for me.[72]

The last chapter of the book inquires into the ontology of the self. The main part of the book developed along the lines of contrasting selfhood with the dialectic of sameness, then the dialectic of otherness. He concludes with a meditation on the kind of ontology entailed by the preliminary conclusions of the hermeneutical self. In other words, Ricoeur began by asking the "what" question, moved to answering the "who" question, and then came back around to reconsider "what" once again. This involves such considerations as the embodied nature of selfhood and the ontological status of otherness within the self. His ruminations here are fascinating, but he indicates that they are only tentative, and they are not central to our concerns, so I will mention them only briefly. On bodiliness, for example, Ricoeur admits that his version of the self has largely left physicality on the fringes. In a suggestive analogy, Ricoeur draws on work from *Time and Narrative* to show that "just as it was necessary to invent the calendar to correlate the lived now with the anonymous instant and to draw up the geographic map to correlate the charnel here with an indifferent place, and thereby to inscribe the proper name—my name—in the civil register, it is necessary, as Husserl himself states, to *make* the flesh *part of the world* (*mondaneiser*) if it is to appear as a body among bodies."[73]

To summarize, I employ a useful reduction formulated by Ricoeur scholar Bernard Dauenhauer, who boils down Ricoeur's relational self to four propositions.

1. Because my personal identity is a narrative identity, I can make sense of myself only in and through my involvement with others.
2. In my dealings with others, I do not simply enact a role or function that has been assigned to me. I can change myself through my own efforts and can reasonably ask others to change as well.
3. Nonetheless, because I am bodily and have inherited both biological and psychological constraints, I cannot change everything about myself and others.
4. Though I can be evaluated in a number of ways, e.g. physical dexterity, verbal fluency, technical skill, the ethical evaluation in the light of my responsiveness to others is, on the whole, the most important evaluation.[74]

Ricoeur's project therefore seems, on the whole, the most successful of the three considered in this chapter in meeting the three desiderata of maintaining individual moral culpability in a relational anthropology. The self is not relational in a merely superficial way, the self's morally evaluable actions are linked determinately to relational self-identity, and culpability is preserved without recourse to a form of faculty anthropology. While Ricoeur's version of the self is not perfect, it does signify a very durable and promising road forward into the as yet imperfectly charted territory of postmodernity.

CHAPTER 6

SOCIAL SIN 2: STRUCTURES OF OPPRESSION

The human is by nature a political animal.
> —*Aristotle, Politics*

Behold, the lamb of God, who takes away the sin of the world.
> —*John 1.29b*

Sin has often been understood as both "state" and "act."[1] Original sin is a state into which all have been born, which leads to individual, actual sins.[2] But this distinction is only supposed to be a helpful way of seeing sin—it is not to be "believed in" for its own sake. When the distinction is made so forcefully that it becomes a separation, then the only contemporary reality that can be named as sinful is a discrete action. And that seems to be too narrow. It restricts the Christian from naming as sin those states of affairs that are plainly contrary to the will, honor, law, or word of God as being "sinful."[3] The degradation of the Earth, systemic sexism and racism, patterns of economic production and consumption that contribute to massive global poverty—these cry out to be called contrary to God's intention for the creation. They therefore count as sin. But what is the relationship between the act and the state of sin in these three examples? Simply driving a car to church pollutes the environment. Environmental degradation on a mass scale is sinful, so do I sin in my daily commute? Simply being nervous when driving through a dangerous and poor part of town at night contributes to feelings of xenophobia and racism. Am I sinning as I worry in my car? Purchasing a car that is made by workers who make less than a sustainable wage contributes to institutionalized poverty. Do I sin in my making my purchase?

The answers to these questions are far from clear. What seems clear is that we need to recover *some* way of analyzing the massive human suffering of our day theologically. That means that we need to have some kind of doctrine of "social sin." The last chapter took the approach of social selfhood, or the "relational self." This chapter takes a different approach by looking at ways of describing social situations, habitual patterns of social relating, and arrangements of power as "structural sin." Here the emphasis is on an analysis of human social networks and human sociality from a theological point of view. Though its social dimension has never been fully excluded from our understanding of sin, it has often been significantly downplayed. In the nineteenth century, Albrecht Ritschl and others tried to recover the language of "kingdom of sin" or "kingdom of evil" to account for widespread human suffering and patterns of diabolical relationships.[4] Walter Rauschenbusch and others proclaimed the "social gospel" that was the proper antidote to "social sin."[5] But the most influential site of theological reflection on social sin in its structural forms has been liberation theology, both in its Latin American and feminist forms.

STRUCTURAL SIN IN LATIN AMERICAN LIBERATION THEOLOGY

The story of liberation theology and its eye-opening analyses of the social-structural dimension of sin has to start with Gustavo Gutiérrez. Born in Lima, Peru, in 1928, Fr. Gutiérrez was educated there and then in Europe, where he earned a doctorate in theology at the University of Lyons. He studied with, and deeply appreciated the learning of, many of the leading lights of European theology of the mid-twentieth century, including Henri de Lubac, Karl Rahner, and his fellow Dominican priest Yves Congar. Yet, in learning from these European theologians, he came to see their thinking as, well, *European*. That is to say, while it was deeply influential on the young Gutiérrez's mind, it was also much more perspectival, partial, and rooted in its own particular presuppositions and needs than it cared to admit. After serving as a "*peritus*" or theological expert advising a bishop, at the Second Vatican Council (1962–5), Gutiérrez came home to his native Peru determined to write theology from the perspective of, and to meet the needs of, his own people. This implied taking a hard look at the unmistakable data of his own context, especially the death-dealing poverty that ravaged South America. In fact, as he worked as a teacher and a parish priest, Gutiérrez came to see virtually all of life and faith along the lines of this massive poverty. Among the few words appropriate to describe such a situation was "sin." And Gutiérrez gives this old word quite new content and shape. His landmark 1971 book *A Theology of Liberation* put many of these thoughts into seminal form.

Many of Gutiérrez's earlier writings, such as the 1968 essay "Toward a Theology of Liberation,"[6] are extremely critical of worldviews whose construals of sin envision sin as nearly totally a *personal* phenomenon, lacking any social dimension, apart from possibly negative social effects of individual sin. Gutiérrez could not disagree more. Gutiérrez counters, "Sin, the breach with God, is not something that occurs only within some intimate sanctuary of the heart. It *always* moves into interpersonal relationships, and hence is the ultimate root of all injustice and oppression—as well as of the social confrontations and conflicts of concrete history."[7] In other words, Gutiérrez claims that for an analysis of sin to be authentic, its two dimensions need to be clarified; it analytically entails a break with God, and synthetically a breach with other persons. This matches with his insistence that sin is always *both* personal and social in nature. Put most simply, Gutiérrez thinks that sin is not simply a matter of the sinful individual's will before God. Whatever must be named as *sin* will never be an act separated from its evil-perpetuating effects in the world. Sinful situations, structures, or social arrangements can never adequately be named as sinful without reference to their root cause in the acts of sinful individuals, but they are nonetheless not reducible to those individual acts, nor are they accordingly any less "real" or "sinful" because they are derivative.

Gutiérrez notes how long this social dimension has been ignored, stating that "There was a period . . . when the predominant type of theology neglected the social dimension of sin. In recent decades a growing awareness of the social problem has brought a return to the true perspective with its profound biblical roots; in addition Medellín brought it to mind when it spoke of a 'sinful situation.'"[8] It might be fair to say that the fervor with which this one-sidedness in traditional formulations of sin has been attacked has caused the pendulum to swing perhaps too far to the social side, leading to a lack of attention paid on individual human sinful actions. Latin American liberation theologians often emphasize the social aspect of sin so strongly that the role of the individual is eclipsed.[9] This is perhaps understandable, for as Gutiérrez rightly claims, "The emphasis on the social dimension of sin [in liberation theology] is due to the fact that this dimension was so little present to Christian consciousness at that time."[10]

Choosing to focus on the social, instead of the personal, dimension to sin is not just sour grapes. Rather "the emphasis is thus placed chiefly because this perspective, based on the faith, enables us to understand better what has happened and what is still happening in Latin America."[11] Statements like this illuminate Gutiérrez's theological method, which can be summarized by the slogan "critical reflection on praxis."[12] "Praxis" means reasoned, self-aware practices. The practices of dealing with the social effects of sin in Latin America confounded efforts to make sense of the actual experiences of the poor. The poor of Gutiérrez's congregation in Lima were not well served by the notions of sin Gutiérrez had studied in Europe. Such emphases as the anxiety an individual experiences when countless choices for a life-direction are available, sexual indiscretion, a temptation toward an absolutized self—these conceptions of sin could make no sense of the dominant factor in Gutiérrez's ministry: institutionalized poverty. Something much deeper was needed.

These, then, are the roots of Gutiérrez's criticism of privatized, individualistic notions of sin. In language resonating with echoes of Marx, Gutiérrez asserts that Christian theology has placed the blame for sin *on the oppressed*, and identified resistance to social arrangements with sin itself. He shows the total separation between individual acts of sin and their experience and proliferation in the social sphere to be a sham. He points out the near impossibility of an act that was sinful (because it was a breach of friendship with God) that did not also have social consequences. Note how this is a different emphasis than the social understanding of sin from the last chapter; there it was because humans must relate to each other that they sin. For Gutiérrez and other liberation theologians, however, it is because humans sin that they relate to each other in sinful contexts, broken patterns, and oppressive structures.

SIN AS STRUCTURES THAT PERPETUATE OPPRESSION

Gutiérrez was one of the major leaders at the Puebla conference of Latin American Bishops in 1979. A document from that gathering contains a clue to Gutiérrez's proposed corrective to the tradition whose shortcomings we have seen: "Sinfulness on the personal level, the break with God that debases the human being, is always *mirrored* on the level of interpersonal relations in a corresponding egotism, haughtiness, ambition, and envy." Further, "These traits produce injustice, domination, violence at every level, and conflicts between individuals, groups, social classes, and peoples. They also produce corruption, hedonism, aggravated sexuality, and superficiality in mutual relations."[13] The social dimension of sin is seen here not as something qualitatively different from sin at its personal level. Haughtiness and arrogance at the level of the individual is mirrored as egotism and domination at the social level. The cumulative effect of acts of violence by sinful individuals is its mirror image, a violent social system. Commenting on this passage, Gutiérrez writes, "All this is a description of a situation of sin, a notion that, as we have already mentioned, was central in Medellín and which Puebla here takes up again with greater force and insistence."[14]

The relationship of personal and social expressions of sin is therefore *causal*. Personal sins cause situations which must be named as sinful. Consider this citation from *A Theology of Liberation*:

> Sin—a breach of friendship with God and others—is according to the Bible the ultimate cause of poverty, injustice, and the oppression in which persons live. In describing sin as the ultimate cause we do not in any way negate the structural reasons and the objective determinants leading to these situations. It does, however, emphasize the fact that things do not happen by chance and that behind an unjust structure there is a personal or collective will responsible—a willingness to reject God and neighbor. It suggests, likewise, that a social transformation, no matter how radical it may be, does not automatically achieve the suppression of all evils.[15]

A possible way of interpreting this position is to see a kind of dialectic of sin at work in passages like this. Such a view would see the sinful acts of individuals as the causes of sinful situations or structures, with those sinful situations or structures then acting back on the sinner in such a way as to perpetuate the sin. But this is not Gutiérrez's position. The structures of sin are not, in Gutiérrez's view, capable of agency. To call them "sinful" is not to say that they sin, for Gutiérrez insists on the derivative nature of sinful structures. Structures cannot act. Structures are not morally evaluable. While Gutiérrez wants to expand the notion of sin from its previously privatized and individualistic myopia, he is extremely careful to maintain the critical link between sin as the acts of persons and the structures which bear the sinful effects of those acts.

Since this is a critical distinction, perhaps some more citations from Gutiérrez will show his caution on this matter. For example, he writes, "Sin is a rejection of the gift of God's love. The rejection is a personal, free act. It is a refusal to accept God as Father and to love others as the Lord loved us. Only the action of God can heal human beings at the root of the egotism that prevents them from going out of themselves."[16] Or again, "The importance of the social consequences of sin does not mean forgetting that sin is always the result of a personal, free act."[17] Sin is primarily understood as an act against God, and derivatively as a failure to love one's neighbor. Because sin is the first, it is also the second, not vice versa.[18] However, love of God and love of one's neighbor are intertwined, for as Gutiérrez writes, "There is no love for God without love for one's brothers and sisters, particularly those who are most poor, and this means . . . a commitment on the level of social structures, 'with all the consequences that will entail on the plane of temporal realities.'"[19] For Gutiérrez, as for many other liberation theologians, human liberation unfolds according to a three-layered scheme, involving political, personal, and religious liberation.[20] The oppressed must first be freed from the unjust social structures which dominate their lives. Following this, there must be a kind of personal transformation "by which we live with a kind of profound inner freedom in the face of every kind of servitude."[21] Finally, there must be a liberation before God from sin. Each level of liberation is intimately connected with each of the other two, so it makes little sense to say that one could have liberation in the religious sphere (and therefore a restoration of love for and friendship with God) without a corresponding liberation in one's interpersonal relations.

Gutiérrez has sometimes been accused of espousing an overly rosy optimism concerning the possibilities for the creation of utopia on earth. This is probably due to the fact that human effort toward liberation on the first two levels, the political and the personal, is both possible and mandated in Gutiérrez's theology. Against his detractors Gutiérrez writes, "In my own approach to theology, sin occupies a central place . . . Because sin is radical evil, it can only be conquered by the grace of God and the radical liberation that the Lord bestows.

The relationship between grace and sin is played out in the inmost depths of the human person."[22] Each of the levels of liberation is effected, finally, by God's gratuitous love; but liberation on the religious level is exclusively God's domain.

One last thing must be said about Gutiérrez's view of sin, and it comes from his critics. Gutiérrez repeatedly states that the logic of sin as he understands it is true across time and space, *and across the oppressed/oppressor dividing line.* That is to say, it is not only those who have political, economic, and social power who abuse that power in sin. The poor are not to be "preferred" because they sin less, but simply because they are poor. Oppressed and oppressor alike sin. The forms their sin might take could vary, and the suffering produced by their sin will certainly vary directly with their potential power. While it is fine to state this, one wonders whether Gutiérrez is really able to account for the differences that forms of sin take in people of such different social strata. As many critics have pointed out, Gutiérrez's rhetoric of oppressor versus oppressed can sometimes seem more like the parsing of a population than the naming of a universal phenomenon.[23]

STRUCTURAL SIN IN FEMINIST THEOLOGY

The beginnings of self-consciously "feminist theology," as opposed to theology simply written by women, lie in the relatively recent past. On the doctrine of sin, we might not need to look much further back than 1960, which saw the publication of Valerie Saiving's seminal article exposing the flagrant androcentrism of Reinhold Niebuhr's doctrine of sin.[24] Saiving took the position that Niebuhr's insistence on the central role of *superbia* (pride) in sinning was simply males' experiences of self-affirmation and high self-regard writ large across the sky as a way of covering all human experience of sin. Saiving noted that excessive pride born of the life of near constant self-transcendent activity was hardly accurate as an articulation of the experience of women. She responded with an account toward what a doctrine of sin might look like based on more equitable gendered experience. Judith Plaskow,[25] Susan Nelson Dunfee,[26] Daphne Hampson,[27] and many others subsequently engaged in similar projects. Yet these approaches are often different ways of describing how individuals sin when viewed from the male versus the female perspective. Other feminists have offered insightful analyses of the way that sin functions at the social level. This chapter concludes with a look at two such thinkers, Elisabeth Schüssler Fiorenza and Ivone Gebara.

Elisabeth Schüssler Fiorenza is a groundbreaking feminist New Testament interpreter. Her 1983 text *In Memory of Her: A Feminist Theological Reconstruction of Christian Origins* is already a classic of theology constructed in close conversation with biblical hermeneutics.[28] In that work Schüssler Fiorenza synthesized traditional methods of biblical study with a brand of feminist "hermeneutics of suspicion" in order to unearth new meanings from several key New Testament texts, as well as texts from the early history of the church. Her general pattern of hermeneutics follows the pattern "suspicion, proclamation, remembrance, and creative actualization."[29] She has uncovered a picture of a community that was more hospitable to women than had ever been imagined. Many had previously asserted that the early Christian perspective on women moved toward equality, but that this shift was a symptom of an imminent Pauline eschatology which made little of *difference* in general (as Gal. 3.28 puts it, neither Greek nor Jew, male nor female, etc.). Schüssler Fiorenza moved past this, arguing that the proclamation of Jesus asserted the full equality of women. As evidence for this conclusion she cites the central roles accorded to women in Jesus's ministry as well as in the early church, in addition to the explicit words of Jesus, and particularly to the scenes in the gospels of the woman who anoints Jesus, whose story should be told where the gospel is proclaimed, "in memory of her." (Mark 14.9 and parallels).[30] Schüssler Fiorenza thus began to see sexism as a *distortion of the structure of society* proclaimed by Jesus to be in accord with God, and was therefore something like "structural sin."[31]

Schüssler Fiorenza uses the word *kyriarchy* to refer to the distorted, top-down power structures of domination and subordination effective in the social and political life in the family and the state.[32] *Kyriarchy* is founded on the notion that the lord, the father, and the master are superior to the subject, the family, and the slave. It is this fact of governance, or even the very existence of such a structure, which then leads to androcentrism (the idea that male human experience is normative) and from there to sexism. Androcentrism is one of the nefarious tools that already sexist communities use to legitimate their use of coercive power in those communities.[33]

The first Christian communities which emerged from Jesus's liberating proclamation differ totally from the "kyriocentric"[34] view one might get from an unnuanced reading of, for example, the "household codes" of Ephesians and Colossians. Schüssler Fiorenza's word for describing the way it really was is *ekklesia*. The *ekklesia* (the word refers to the church, but etymologically it means "the ones who are called to be together") is a way of organizing human relationships without any hierarchy, patriarchy, or *kyriarchy*. It is utterly egalitarian in all its social manifestations.[35] But more than an intellectual concept, the *ekklesia* functions for Schüssler Fiorenza as an eminently practical location of social interaction that is not a distortion of Jesus's message and historical praxis. "[E]kklesia comes through the agency of the Spirit to visible, tangible expression in and through the gathering of God's people around the table, eating together, a meal, breaking the bread, and sharing the cup in memory of Christ's passion and resurrection." This implies, further, "eating together, sharing together, drinking together, talking with each other, receiving each other, experiencing God's presence through each other, and in doing so, proclaiming the gospel as Gods alternative vision for everyone, especially for those who are poor, outcast, and battered."[36] This could be read as a kind of way of talking about sin and its overcoming. *Kyriarchy* is the diagnosis, and *ekklesia* the prescription. Schüssler Fiorenza only uses the term "structural sin" a handful of times in her writings and does not invest it with significant content.[37] But many women, writing from the perspective of normative theology rather than descriptive critical-historical work in ancient Christianity, have taken Schüssler Fiorenza's cue and developed her lines of analysis into actual sin-talk. While it may in fact be self-evident that *kyriarchy* is to be opposed on the grounds that it is oppressive to women, most feminist systematic theologians have gone a significant step further than this and argued that such oppressive social structures are properly sinful because they are against God as well as women.[38]

One feminist thinker who has taken Schüssler Fiorenza's notion of structures of domination further is the Brazilian philosophical theologian Ivone Gebara. Gebara, like Schüssler Fiorenza, focuses on eminently practical understandings of religious life in her writing. In the same vein as Schüssler Fiorenza's reconstruction of women's experience in the early *ekklesia* of Christianity, Gebara's work tends to be concrete and practical when it comes to discussing sin.[39] Gebara encounters in women's experience of evil a confusing mixture of evil's transcendence and immanence.[40] Evil is at once a grand overarching concept within which reflective people interpret their lives, and yet also much more familiar and immediate. It is, in sum, exceedingly *domestic*. Gebara employs a phenomenological method[41] in approaching evil that brackets out consideration of the overarching concept of Evil temporarily, the better to remain concrete in her analysis of evils.[42] In this way, evil can be seen as something as simple as the horrifying reality experienced by women whom Gebara knows are forced to say: "Today I was lucky. There was a lot of trash in the streets." Gebara laments that "Collecting trash confers the power to eat: who among the politicians would set the standard so low?"[43] There is also the mundane but daily pain of having soap but not water, or water but no soap.[44] Gebara is pointing out that in Latin American women's experience, evil is not so much *interpreted* as it is immediately and immanently experienced. Thus Gebara wants us to focus not on a kind of cosmic account of Evil, but on the very domestic, palpable and mundane *evils* which all people, particularly women, experience every day.[45]

This last statement hints at the structural dimensions of human evil. There is something about the way the question of evil and sin has been posed by male theologians and philosophers that has, in turn, actually *contributed to* and *exacerbated* the evils that women experience. Dominant theology has relied too much on dualistic categories which understand men as created good and women as incarnate fallen evil.[46] Following Rosemary Radford Ruether's thought, Gebara maintains that this denigration of women as embodied evil manifests itself not only in acts of sin committed against women, but also in the denigration of the natural environment. In fact, in another work Gebara explicitly explores the links between a growing ecological awareness and the liberation (particularly, but not only) of women.[47]

Gebara is aware that her emphasis on women's experience of evil could make it appear that she is blind to the sins women commit. She quotes a haunting passage from Zygmunt Bauman, who writes, "As a rule, victims are not ethically superior to their victimizers; what makes them seem morally better, and makes credible their claim to this effect, is the fact that—being weaker—they have had less opportunity to commit cruelty."[48] Gebara thus asserts that she can "detect in some way, directly or indirectly, that they [women who experience evil] have also themselves committed immoral acts."[49] Since women in Latin America are rarely allowed into the kinds of positions of power where they could contribute to the creation of systems of domination, in their own way they acquiesce to them and further their sinful ends. The youngest daughter of some Mexican families, for example, is not allowed to marry in order that she be free to care for her parents in their old age. The mother is often viciously cruel in enforcing this "structure of evil" that harms her daughter.[50] Mothers tell their daughters not to be like the "prostitutes, single mothers, black and indigenous women, and lesbians" present in their communities.[51] The power of evil makes itself known most when those who suffer most from it make it stronger by remaining in it. Yet Gebara's reflections on evil are also deeply rooted in the hope borne of the equally domestic, equally concrete experiences of salvation of the women among whom she lives,[52] as well as hope in what she elsewhere calls "women's collective power."[53]

Gebara's work represents a powerful effort to engage the roots of the experience of evil (dualisms, binary oppositions, the identity of women with "nature" and the denigration of both) and the concrete phenomenology of that experience. Mysterious forces, learned behaviors, inherited sexist conceptual schemes and, quite simply, the social inertia of the status quo work together to condition humans both to construct and to comply with structures that perpetuate evil. The social dimension of sin thus involves not just the fact that sinful people emerge from contexts of distorted relationships (Chapter 5), but that phenomena genuinely *outside* of human selves, like legal systems, theological concepts, and patterns of commerce and politics, can contribute to *states of affairs* that are profoundly contrary to God's intentions, and yet are not easily reduced to their constituent sinful *actions*. Thus a full notion of sin in its social dimensions would require attention both to the sin inherent in relational selfhood and to the sin implicit in structures that harm and oppress God's good creation.

CONCLUSION

Human nature remains good, even "after the fall." Human nature is one thing, and sin is another thing.[1] To be a human is to be good, but also to be prone to weakness, fault, and sin. The foregoing chapters have come at this tendency in a variety ways. Let me attempt one final theme by way of conclusion. Human sin emerges when violations of "soil" and "spirit" occur. Settling too far into our "earthiness" and being less than we are called to be leads to sin. Asserting ourselves in our self-transcendent mode of spirit also leads to sin.

The English word "human" comes from the Latin word "homo," as in *homo sapiens*, which in turn comes from the word "humus." And humus means soil. In a very real sense, to be a human is to be of the earth. We rely on the earth for our sustenance, and we share its elements and basic chemistry. We speak of a person who is an authentic self as being "salt of the earth" or "earthy." The biblical witness illuminates this connection between the ground and human beings. The Hebrew word for human, *adam*, is closely related to the word for soil, *adamah*. In one of the critical texts for theological anthropology, Genesis 2.7, we read, "then the Lord God formed man from the dust of the ground, and breathed into his nostrils the breath of life; and the man became a living being." The human—and here "Adam" does not refer to one specific person so much as human beings in general—is literally formed from humus, from soil.[2] Feet planted firmly on the ground from which we came, to be a human being is to have much in common with the rest of creation. What is our source is also our end; as a later verse in Genesis puts it, "By the sweat of your face you shall eat bread until you return to the ground, for out of it you were taken; you are dust, and to dust you shall return" (Gen. 3.19). The human is exhumed—taken out of the humus. One virtue of humanity is humility, which might be described as being rooted to the earth, aware of and nurtured by one's roots.

It is not just the OT that remarks on the close connection between human and humus. In ancient Greek mythology, Pyrrha and her husband Deucalion are tasked with repopulating the Earth after a great flood. They throw stones over their shoulders as they walk below Mount Parnassus, and when the stones land, they slowly turn into humans. An early commentator on this story identifies the word for people, *laoi*, with the word for a stone, *laas*.[3] An ancient Babylonian and Akkadian myth, the *Enuma Elish*, recounts the creation of humans by the god Marduk from the blood of the slain god Kingu being mixed with clay.[4]

How does sin relate to the human as soil? The human can succumb to being *less* than one is called to be. Karl Barth called this the sin of sloth. Reinhold Niebuhr called it the sin of sensuality. Humans have much in common with the rest of creation, but they cannot succumb to being *only* an animal. It is natural, for example, for male whitetail deer to try to inseminate as many females as they are able. It is natural for male bighorn sheep to beat their male rivals to the point of death. Not knowing when the next meal might come, some animals eat exorbitant amounts when food happens to be available. Parenting habits of animals vary widely, to the point of leaving offspring to fend for themselves immediately after birth. Yet Christianity rightly would call such behaviors "sins" when done by humans. While there is and ought to be continuity between the human being and the rest of creation, the overlap of behavior between humans and nonhuman creatures cannot be total.

However, humans aren't just soil, they're also spirit. Humans have the capacity for self-transcendence. Humans have free will. Humans have souls. A central affirmation Christians make with respect to theological anthropology is that humans are created in the image of God. The *imago Dei* implies that humans are gifted by God in particular ways, and thus bear a special burden in the care of creation. It affirms that humans are created in the image of God in a way that other creatures are not. The answers given to the question "What do humans have that other creatures do not that gives them the *imago Dei*?" are numerous. Some have said that this is language. Others have said that humans have a rational soul, and this is what the *imago Dei* refers to.[5] Consciousness, conscience, and even walking upright[6] have been held up as possible referents of the *imago Dei*. Whatever the image refers to, it is not lost in sin. The mirror onto which the image is cast is caked with the grime of sin and coated with a film of ignorance, but the image itself is still visible.

How does sin relate to the human as spirit? The human can claim to be *more* than one is called to be. Barth, Niebuhr, and a whole host of others call this the sin of pride, not in a superficially psychological sense of an overly high personal estimation, but rather the self-assertion of a creature who would seek to take the place of the creator. Such prideful rebellion can take a number of forms. Seeking to secure our own future, we can greedily amass excessive wealth and power, such that trust in God becomes moot as we trust ourselves entirely. When one proudly sees oneself in control of a business, family, or nation, then lying or cheating to maintain control soon seems to be justified. We can implicitly claim to be so righteous as to not need salvation, or indeed any assistance whatsoever. As William Placher notes, "We set ourselves up as if we could decide for ourselves the purposes of our lives, as if we were the masters of our fates and the captains of our souls."[7]

This book started with a recommendation both of sin as a moral vocabulary and of perplexity as an orientation to sin. One does not want to claim to be able to explain *too well* something that, by its nature, is unexplainable. The edges of sin should be sharpened, not dulled, by Christian theology. But the theologian also must not claim to say too little about something as central to the gospel as is an understanding of sin, especially in days such as the present, when sin is either a caricature or a museum artifact. To be perplexed at sin is better than to be unaware of it. The foregoing chapters have heralded sin as good news, perhaps best understood as the denial of God's word. Its biblical bases were explored in their many forms, as were ways that sin has been problematized in modern critical thought. Though the one thing is thus described in countless ways, still it is just one thing—that which is *against God*. To understand it, then, is no more difficult, nor easier, than knowing God's own self.

NOTES

CHAPTER 1

1 A recent provocative and insightful attempt to show that the language of sin more adequately accounts for such evils as the Holocaust and child abuse comes from Alistair McFadyen, *Bound to Sin: Abuse, Holocaust, and the Christian Doctrine of Sin* (Cambridge: Cambridge University Press, 2000).

2 Kierkegaard, *Fear and Trembling* in *Søren Kierkegaard Skrifter* 4:154–5.

3 Unerringly reliable in its approach to evil along these lines is Marilyn McCord Adams, *Horrendous Evils and the Goodness of God* (Ithaca, NY: Cornell University Press, 1999) and idem, *Christ and Horrors: The Coherence of Christology* (Cambridge: Cambridge University Press, 2006).

4 *CD* III/3, 319, trans. altered.

5 I first heard the matter put this way by Eric Dean, *The Good News about Sin: Sermons Preached in the Wabash College Chapel* (Crawfordsville, IN: Wabash College, 1982), and my thanks go to Raymond B. Williams for calling the book to my attention.

6 Of course there is more overlap between the categories than this schema makes it appear; God wills the right treatment of neighbor, so in at least a derivative sense, mistreatment of neighbor is sinful.

7 Stephen H. Webb, Review of James Morone, *Hellfire Nation: The Politics of Sin in American History*, in *Conversations in Religion and Theology* 4 (2006), 2:166.

8 A persuasive and entertaining case to this effect is made in John Portmann, *A History of Sin: Its Evolution to Today and Beyond* (Lanham, MD: Rowman and Littlefield, 2007).

9 A lucid portrayal not of the eclipse but of the migration of sin among academic theologians is offered by David H. Kelsey, "Whatever Became of the Doctrine of Sin?" *Theology Today* 50 (1993):2, 169–78.

10 Karl Menninger, *Whatever Became of Sin?* (New York: Hawthorn, 1972).

11 For example, see the effort of the Evangelical Lutheran Church in America's *Renewing Worship* initiative, which found numerous ways to speak of "falling short" of God's will, or "erring" with good intentions.

12 William James, *The Varieties of Religious Experience* (New York: Penguin, 1985), 91.

13 Richard Dawkins, *The God Delusion* (New York: Houghton Mifflin, 2006), 285.

14 Alexander Pope, *Essay on Man and Satires* (Middlesex: Echo, 2007), 15.

15 The Vatican II document *Gaudium et Spes* makes unequivocal statements about slavery being sinful in paragraphs 27–9. Though this document is from 1965, earlier statements had been made in the nineteenth century and even before. Still, the influence of Thomas Aquinas, who said that slavery could neither be defended nor condemned under the natural law, contributed to a fairly equivocal position taken toward slavery. See Stephen F. Brett, *Slavery and the Catholic Tradition: Rights in the Balance* (New York: Peter Lang, 1994).

16 Clement, *The Instructor*, 2.10.91.

17 Clement, *Stromata*, 3.7.

18 Clement, *The Instructor*, 2.10.95.

19 All data are taken from a press release from United Nations, Department of Economic and Social Affairs, Population Division, "World Marriage Data, 2008."

20 This refers to a kind of argumentation wherein one side of a dispute is required to articulate the case of the opponent in such a way that the opponent says, "Yes, that is what I am saying."

21 Alisdair MacIntyre, *After Virtue* (South Bend, IN: University of Notre Dame Press, 1984), 168.

22 A splendid introduction to preaching as truth telling can be found in Frederick Buechner, *Telling the Truth: The Gospel as Tragedy, Comedy and Fairy Tale* (New York: Harper and Row, 1977).

23 *Cur Deus Homo*, 1.11.2.

24 *Cur Deus Homo*, 1.11.3.

25 *Cur Deus Homo*, 1.11.3.

26 John Calvin, *Institutes of the Christian Religion*, trans. John McNeill (Louisville, KY: Westminster John Knox, 1960), 35.

27 On this point, see the searching essay of Belden C. Lane, "Spirituality as the Performance of Desire: Calvin's Metaphor of the World as a Theatre of God's Glory," *Spiritus* 1:1(2001), 1–30.

28 Calvin, *Institutes*, 188.

29 Calvin, *Institutes*, 252.

30 Calvin, *Institutes*, 245.

31 See B. A. Gerrish, "The Mirror of God's Goodness: Man in the Theology of John Calvin," in *Concordia Theological Quarterly* 45:3 (1981): 212.

32 Calvin, *Institutes*, 251. On this matter, see above all Thomas F. Torrance, *Calvin's Doctrine of Man* (London: Lutterworth, 1949); also Don H. Compier, *John Calvin's Rhetorical Doctrine of Sin* (New York: Mellen, 2001) and Mary Potter Engel, *John Calvin's Perspectival Anthropology* (Eugene, OR: Wipf and Stock, 2002).

33 See Michael L. Czapkay Sudduth, "The Prospects for Mediate Natural Theology in John Calvin," in *Religious Studies* 31 (1995): 53–68, and, for a very different perspective, T. H. L. Parker, *Calvin's Doctrine of the Knowledge of God* (Grand Rapids, MI: Eerdmans, 1959).

34 William Bouwsma is a reliable guide on such matters. See his *John Calvin: A Sixteenth Century Portrait* (New York: Oxford University Press, 1989).

35 B. A. Gerrish, *Grace and Gratitude: The Eucharistic Theology of John Calvin* (Minneapolis: Fortress, 1993).

36 One of the implications of this fixation on order is his sexual anthropology. While Calvin seems to have been less overtly misogynistic in his writings than were other Reformation and Late Medieval writers, the mark of androcentrism is unmistakable. Calvin decried any practice seen to show men as effeminate, and forbade women from wearing overly mannish dress. Following the order created in the natural law meant retaining purity, and that required firm boundaries, especially between the sexes. (Bouwsma notes dozens and dozens of similar texts in Calvin comparing sin to impurity, filth, and disorder.) Rosemary Ruether notes three distinct "statuses" of women in Calvin's anthropology: women have equality with men in that their soul is *imago Dei*, but women are externally subjugated politically (God's order demanding this), and are subjugated in the household to the men in their lives due to the fall (postlapsarian women are forced into this subjugation, which would otherwise have been "voluntary"). See her *Women and Redemption: A Theological History* (Minneapolis: Fortress Press, 1998), 122–4.

37 Luther's and Calvin's followers had difficulty reconciling their teachings on the uses of the law. In Luther's theology, the law served primarily a negative function. The first use of the law was theological: if you have a law, then you know what counts as a transgression of that law, so you know what is sinful. The law also has a civil use: in this crazy, sinful world, having a few rules around can help keep otherwise unruly people in check. Though Luther never (as far as I know) insisted that these were the only possible uses for the law, many of his followers were very nervous about Calvin's addition of a third use. Calvin thought that well-meaning people could use the law as a kind of benchmark for their moral rectitude. Though they would never become fully able to cease violating the law, their transgressions could at least be less frequent and less severe.

38 For a rich and creative example of the polyvalence of "word" and "voice" in Christian theology, see Stephen H. Webb, *The Divine Voice: Christian Proclamation and the Theology of Sound* (Grand Rapids, MI: Brazos, 2004).

39 The affinities of Luther's and Calvin's positions are obvious. Less known is that Luther still does make room for seeing sin as the dishonoring of God. See WA 6:220, WA 18:742, LW 12:309, LW 2:125–6.

40 WA 39.23.

41 LW 34:156.

42 LW 35:369.

43 WA 31:148.

44 See Randall Zachmann, *The Assurance of Faith: Conscience in the Theology of Martin Luther and John Calvin* (Minneapolis: Fortress, 1993).

45 He does not use the expression as often as one might surmise, given how central it is said to be to his hamartiology. He uses it mostly in his lectures on Romans (WA 56.304.26, 56.356.5).

46 Wolfhart Pannenberg, *Anthropology in Theological Perspective*, trans. Matthew J. O'Connell (Louisville, KY: Westminster John Knox, 1989), 71. Luther uses the phrase "*extra se in Christo*" to refer to the natural center that the Christian has in Christ, and making unnatural the self-centeredness of sin. See Wilfried Joest, *Ontologie der Person bei Luther* (Göttingen: Vandenhoeck and Ruprecht, 1967), 273–4.

47 Paul Althaus, *The Theology of Martin Luther*, trans. Robert C. Schulz (Philadelphia: Fortress, 1966), 149.

48 WA 7.25.26ff., WA. 401.443.23ff. See also *Luther's Letters of Spiritual Counsel*, ed. and trans. T. G. Tappert (Philadelphia: Westminster, 1960), 110.

49 Thomas Aquinas, *Summa Theologica* II.1.72.6, emphasis added.

50 *Catechism of the Catholic Church*, 8.1.1849.

51 Jason E. Vickers, *Wesley: A Guide for the Perplexed* (London: Continuum, 2009), 93.

CHAPTER 2

1 Readers wishing to study in greater detail the dizzying number of ways in which "sin" functions in the Bible might start with some of these up-to-date, high-quality texts: Jonathan Klawens, *Impurity and Sin in Ancient Judaism* (New York: Oxford University Press, 2000); Mark J. Boda, *A Severe Mercy: Sin and Its Remedy in the Old Testament* (Winona Lake, IN: Eisenbrauns, 2009); Gary Anderson, *Sin: A History* (New Haven: Yale University Press, 2009); and, since Anderson more or less ignores Paul, Victor Paul Furnish, *Theology and Ethics in Paul*, rev. ed. (Louisville, KY: Westminster John Knox, 2009), 135–61.

2 Hereafter, OT.

3 See, for example, Wendy Doniger Flaherty, *The Origins of Evil in Hindu Mythology* (Berkeley: University of California Press, 1976), 168–72.

4 See "Sin" in *Baker Theological Dictionary of the Bible*, ed. Walter A. Elwell (Grand Rapids, MI: Baker Books, 2001), 745–7.

5 See, for example, Bruce M. Metzger, *An Introduction to the Apocrypha* (New York: Oxford University Press, 1977), 81–9 and 122–4.

6 For more on this, see G. Johannes Botterweck, Helmer Ringgren, and Heinz-Josef Fabry, eds., *Theological Dictionary of the Old Testament* (Grand Rapids, MI: Eerdmans, 1999), 10.549–52; and Gary Anderson, *Sin: A History* (New Haven: Yale University Press, 2009), ch. 2.

7 On this, cf. William W. Hallo, "Biblical Abominations and Sumerian Taboos," *Jewish Quarterly Review* 76 (1985):21–40.

8 Jacob Milgrom discusses this at length in his essay, "The Concept of ma'al in the Bible and the Ancient Near East." *Journal of the American Oriental Society* 96 (1976):236–47.

9 On the creation story and sin, I continue to learn from Conrad Hyers, *The Meaning of Creation: Genesis and Modern Science* (Louisville, KY: Westminster John Knox, 1984) and Dietrich Bonhoeffer, *Creation and Fall: A Theological Exposition of Genesis 1–3*, trans. Douglas Stephen Bax (Minneapolis: Fortress, 1997).

10 Reference must be made here to the outstanding book of James Alison, *Raising Abel: The Recovery of the Eschatological Imagination* (New York: Crossroad, 1996). Alison reads the story of Cain and Abel through the lens of René Girard's philosophy of mimesis and violence. Girard's work, and its significance for a doctrine of sin, will be discussed at length in Chapter 4.

11 Gen. 6.5–6 comes from the Jahwist text, which dates to about 1000–900 BC. The "Adamic covenant" was perhaps not understood to have been given until Hosea, who wrote in the mid-eighth century BC. Hosea 6.7 reads, "But with Adam they transgressed the covenant; there they dealt faithlessly with me."

12 On this notion, see the extensive treatment by Lyle Eslinger, "A Contextual Identification of the bene ha'elohim and benoth ha'adam in Genesis 6:1–4," in *Journal for the Study of the Old Testament* 13 (July 1979): 65–73.

13 The one other place where scholars have detected a hint of culpability for sin in the divine being is Genesis 4.7, where God seemingly dangles sin in front of Cain: "If you do well, will you not be accepted? And if you do not do well, sin is lurking at the door; its desire is for you, but you must master it."

14 For a recent critique of ways that *creatio ex nihilo* has been misused in theologies of creation, in ways that underwrite and retroactively justify colonialist oppression, see the outstanding work of Whitney Bauman, *Theology, Creation and Environmental Ethics: From* Creatio Ex Nihilo *to* Terra Nullius (New York: Routledge, 2009).

15 The phrase occurs in Judges 2.11, 3.12, 4.1, 6.1, 10.6, 13.1, and again in 1 Kings 11.6.

16 It is interesting to note the parallels between this basic view and Paul's understanding of sin in Rom. 14.9, "Whatever does not proceed from faith is sin." Paul fairly rarely cites the prophets in his own theology. Exceptions to this are present, for example, in Paul's usage of Isaiah in Rom. 10.20 and of Hosea in Rom. 9.25.

17 Walther Eichrodt, *Theology of the Old Testament*, trans. John Baker (Philadelphia: Fortress, 1967), 2.383.

18 Amos is described as speaking from the temple of Bethel in Amos 7.13. By calling this imagery to mind, I do not mean to say that such a speech necessarily happened, nor that Amos himself would have included the oracle against Judah, which many scholars claim is an addition from the sixth century BC. I am simply drawing on the canonical shape of Amos as it reads in its present form.

19 Amos 2.6–8, NRSV.

20 John H. Walton, et al., eds., *The IVP Bible Background Commentary* (Downer's Grove, IL: Intervarsity Press, 2000), 551.

21 For example, see Proverbs 6.16–19; 26.25, 3.32; 11.20; 12.22; 15.8, 9, 26; and 17.15. Robin C. Cover discusses sin in the wisdom writings more fully in *Anchor Bible Dictionary*, ed. David Freedman (New Haven, CT: Yale University Press, 1992), 6.38–9, as does K. van der Toorn, *Sin and*

Sanction in Israel and Mesopotamia: A Comparative Study (Assen, Netherlands: Van Gorcum, 1985), 18–20.

22 On this, see also Job 21.17–26.

23 Hereafter, NT.

24 Many have associated this woman with sexual impropriety, though Luke does not state this. Sharon Ringe has noted that the woman's unbound hair (not common in NT times) and her jar of ointment, which could have been part of a "massage" treatment, imply that the woman is a prostitute. See her *Luke* (Louisville, KY: Westminster John Knox, 1995), 108.

25 E. P. Sanders articulates this view in "Sin/Sinners, NT" in David Freedman, ed., *Anchor Bible Dictionary* (New York: Doubleday/Anchor, 1992), 6:31–47.

26 Joachim Jeremias was influential in promoting this view. See his *New Testament Theology: The Proclamation of Jesus* (New York: Scribners, 1971), 109–12, and also *Jerusalem in the Time of Jesus*, (Philadelphia: Fortress, 1969), 105.

27 On this matter one could spend years reading. Good places to begin are: Troels Engberg-Pedersen, *Paul and the Stoics* (Louisville, KY: Westminster John Knox, 2000); Walter Schmitals, *Paul and the Gnostics* (Nashville: Abingdon, 1972); Elaine Pagels, *Gnostic Paul: Gnostic Exegesis of the Pauline Letters* (Harrisburg: Trinity, 1992); David E. Fredrickson, "Ephesians and Stoic Physics" in *Word and World* 22:2 (2002), 144–54; and, more generally, J. Paul Sampley, *Paul in the Greco-Roman World: A Handbook* (New York: Continuum, 2003).

28 No matter how short the duration of the period of such fulfillment or how low the expectations so fulfilled.

29 For this way of putting the matter, I am deeply indebted to the exposition of Victor Paul Furnish, *Theology and Ethics in Paul*, 139–44.

30 See Joseph Healy, "Repentance" in *Anchor Bible Dictionary*, ed. David Freedman (New Haven: Yale University Press, 1992), 4:138–41.

31 See, for example, exponent of the "new perspective" on Paul, such as James D. G. Dunn, *The Theology of Paul the Apostle* (Grand Rapids, MI: Eerdmans, 1998), 70–3; and E. P. Sanders, *Paul and Palestinian Judaism* (Minneapolis: Fortress, 1977), 18, 115, 216. My approach to the "new perspective" is generally in keeping with Karl Donfried, "Paul and the Revisionists: Did Luther Really Get Paul Wrong?" in *Dialog: A Journal of Theology* 46:1 (2007), 31–40.

CHAPTER 3

1 Paul Ricoeur, *The Symbolism of Evil*, trans. Emerson Buchanan (Boston: Beacon, 1986), 178–9, emphasis added.

2 On the rather complicated technical distinction, see the lucid work by Ronnie J. Rombs, *Saint Augustine and the Fall of the Soul: Beyond O'Connell and His Critics* (Washington, DC: Catholic University Press, 2006).

3 *De Gen. ad litt.* 10.19, and letter 166 to Jerome.

4 *De lib. Arb.* 3.1 and *C. Iul.* 5.14.51. See above, n. 2.

5 *The Sayings of the Desert Fathers* 3, 33.
6 *The Sayings of the Desert Fathers*, 7, 9.
7 *The Sayings of the Desert Fathers*, 5.
8 *On the Incarnation of the Word*, 5–7, 13–14, 54.
9 Tertullian, *Exhortation to Chastity*, 2.2.
10 Cyprian of Carthage, *Epistles* 64, 58.5.
11 *Conf.* 1.11.
12 See the fascinating account of this kind of racism in Dorothea Weber, "Some Literary Aspects of the Debate between Julian of Eclanum and Augustine," in *Studia Patristica* 43 (2006): 289–302.
13 *Conf.* 2.4.
14 William C. Placher, *A History of Christian Theology* (Louisville, KY: Westminster John Knox, 1983), 112.
15 Ambrose learned Neoplatonism from Simplicianus, who had in turned studied with Victorianus.
16 *Conf.* 10.29.
17 *Retr.* 1.12.4.
18 *De Gen. ad litt.* 8.25.
19 *De corr. et gr.* 32.
20 *De civ. Dei* 13.20.
21 *De corr. et gr.* 33.
22 *De pecc. mer. et remiss.* 2.36, and *De civ. Dei.* 14.11.
23 *De civ. Dei.* 12.8.
24 *De corr. et gr.* 34.
25 *De civ. Dei.* 14.12.
26 *De mor. eccl. cath.* I.xxii.40, quoted in Peter Brown, *Augustine of Hippo* (Berkeley: University of California Press, 1967), 388.
27 *De lib. arb.* 3.2.
28 *C. Iul.* 6.22 and 3.57.
29 *De nupt. et conc,* 2.15.
30 *De pecc. mer. et remiss.* 3.14.
31 *Retr.* 1.13.5.
32 *De civ. Dei,* 22.24. Augustine is quoting Psalm 49.20.
33 *De trin.* 14.4.
34 *De trin.* 14.8.11.
35 On this point, and on many others made in this chapter, the reader is referred to the fine essay of Jesse Couenhoven, "St. Augustine's Doctrine of Original Sin," in *Augustinian Studies* 36:2 (2005) 359–96.
36 See Gerald Bonner, *St. Augustine of Hippo: Life and Controversies* (Philadelphia: Westminster Press, 1963), 371–2.
37 *Ser.* 151.5.
38 Peter Brown, *Augustine of Hippo*, 388, paraphrasing Augustine, *Ser.* 151.4.
39 *De nupt. et concup.* 1.24.27.
40 *C. Iul.* 4.2.10 and 6.18.56.
41 Actually, this phrase was added along with several others by the Council of Constantinople in 381 AD, which expanded the original creed of the 325 AD Council of Nicaea. Augustine would have known both texts.

42 *Conf.* 1.7. Much recent scholarship in neuroscience and developmental psychology has corroborated Augustine's insight that the formation of moral ideas and standards happens much earlier than many might think. See, for example, William F. Arsenio and Elizabeth A. Lemerise, eds., *Emotions, Aggression and Morality in Children: Bridging Development and Psychopathology* (Washington, DC: American Psychological Association, 2010).

43 *De nupt. et conc.* 1.22.

44 Of the myriad places to which I could point readers on this matter, a particularly lucid example is William C. Placher, "Struggling with Scripture," in Walter Brueggemann, Brian K. Blout, and William C. Placher, *Struggling with Scripture* (Louisville, KY: Westminster John Knox, 2002), 32–50.

45 *De civ. Dei.* 12.10.

46 For example, see Henry McHenry, "Human Evolution," in Michael Ruse, Joseph Travis, and E. O. Wilson, eds. *Evolution: The First Four Billion Years* (Cambridge, MA: Belknap Press of Harvard University Press, 2005), 256–80.

47 The difficulty of explaining the origin of Cain's wife played an important role in the Scopes Trial, where Clarence Darrow's interrogation of William Jennings Bryant pressed Bryant to account for the apparent non-historicity of Genesis. Leslie Allen, ed., *Darrow and Bryan at Dayton* (New York: A. Lee and Company, 1925), 74–5. Carl Sagan's book *Contact*, and the Robert Zemeckis film of the same name, describes the difficulty of Ellie, a scientist, to come to terms with the historicity of Genesis. Sagan, *Contact* (New York: Pocket Books, 1985), 19–20.

48 Rom 6.22–3, NRSV.

49 "After" can here mean not only "chronologically following," but also "ontologically consequent to" or "logically contingent upon."

50 Though if the world economic scene does not improve soon, many of us may not be able to retire until we've reached a ripe old age!

51 Eph 2.1–2, NRSV.

52 Wisdom of Solomon 2.23–4, NRSV.

53 Niebuhr, *Nature and Destiny of Man* (New York: Charles Scribner's Sons, 1941), 1:173–4.

54 *Adv. haer.* 3.22.

55 *Sel. in Ex.* 17.17.

56 *Par.* 42.

57 Homilies on Timothy, 9. Tatha Wiley and Kris Kvam compile similar, though longer lists. See Wiley, *Original Sin: Origins, Developments, Contemporary Meanings* (New York: Paulist, 2002), 171–3; and Kvam, et al., *Eve and Adam: Jewish, Christian and Muslim Readings on Genesis and Gender* (Bloomington: Indiana University Press, 1999), 128–55.

58 Susan Nelson Dunfee, "The Sin of Hiding: A Feminist Critique of Reinhold Niebuhr's Account of the Sin of Pride," *Soundings* 65 (1982): 316–27.

59 William Sloane Coffin, *Credo* (Louisville, KY: Westminster John Knox Press, 2004), 147. Similar statements occur on pp. 6 and 33.

60 *New England Primer*, 1777 edition.

61 Jonathan Edwards, *Original Sin* (New Haven: Yale University Press, 1970), 222.
62 See the excellent work by Gerald McDermott, *Understanding Jonathan Edwards: An Introduction to America's Theologian* (New York: Oxford University Press, 2003), 154–6.
63 Edwards, *Original Sin*, 389.
64 Alan Jacobs, *Original Sin: A Cultural History* (New York: HarperOne, 2008), ch. 9.

CHAPTER 4

1 My understanding of the ways in which synonyms and "root metaphors" function to expand or narrow the imaginative field of a concept, especially a theological one like sin, has been heavily influenced by George Lakoff and Mark Johnson, *Metaphors We Live By* (Chicago: University of Chicago Press, 1980). This chapter concludes with more thoughts on how Lakoff's and Johnson's work helps us make sense of the multiplicity of synonyms for sin.
2 In Stanley Hauerwas, *Truthfulness and Tragedy: Further Investigations into Christian Ethics* (Notre Dame, IN: Notre Dame University Press, 1977), 127–31.
3 To see this notion developed more, one could investigate contemporary anthropologies based, at least in part, on Hegel, for example Merold Westphal, *Hegel, Freedom and Modernity* (Albany, NY: SUNY Press, 1992) and Mark C. Taylor, *Journeys to Selfhood: Hegel and Kierkegaard* (Berkeley: University of California Press, 1980).
4 From the NRSV.
5 We must be careful when interpreting passages like this not to fall victim to the tendency to read atavistically. Paul did not have "the introspective conscience" that Krister Stendahl notes has characterized later eisegesis of the Apostle's writings. Yet is clear that Paul thinks of some kind of fundamental conflict, or estrangement, lying at the core of human existence. Krister Stendahl, "The Apostle Paul and the Introspective Conscience of the West," *Harvard Theological Review* 56 (1963), 199–215. Stendahl's essay on psychology is to be taken seriously despite the fact that he praises Erik Erikson's awful and completely discredited biography of Luther in its pages!
6 On Tillich's thought in general, see the excellent contribution in this series, Andrew O'Neill, *Tillich: A Guide for the Perplexed* (London and New York: T&T Clark, 2008).
7 Paul Tillich, *Systematic Theology* (Chicago: University of Chicago Press, 1957), vol. 2, 29–43.
8 Tillich, *Systematic Theology* (Chicago: University of Chicago Press, 1951), vol. 1, 174–86. Hereafter ST with volume and page number.
9 This is essentially what the existentialist philosopher Martin Heidegger referred to as *Geworfenheit* or "thrown-ness." Heidegger, *Being and Time*, trans. Joan Stambaugh (Albany, NY: SUNY Press, 1996), 134–7, and many other passages.

10 ST II, 33.

11 ST II, 30.

12 I prescind here from a discussion on the finer points of the debates surrounding the authorship of these books. At the very least, one can say that there is a consistent theology present in these books, even if they were created more by a "school of thought" than by one author. For a good introduction to the salient points of contention, see Robert R. Wilson, "Who Was the Deuteronomist? (Who Was Not the Deuteronomist?): Reflections on Pan-Deuteronomism," in *Those Elusive Deuteronomists: "Pan-Deuteronomism" and Scholarship in the Nineties*, ed. Linda Schearing and Steven L. McKenzie (Sheffield: JSOT Press, 1999), 67–82.

13 A particularly telling use of the phrase can be found in the text most closely associated with David, Psalm 23. There is a chiasm in this text, such that the exact midpoint of the psalm is the phrase translated as "for you are with me" (Ps. 23.4b).

14 One view on this can be found in Walter Brueggemann, *The Prophetic Imagination*, 2nd ed. (Minneapolis: Fortress, 2001), 24–6.

15 The indebtedness to Barth is here unmistakable. For a brilliant censure of the *homo faber* concept, see also Nicholas Wolterstorff, *Until Justice and Peace Embrace* (Grand Rapids, MI: Eerdmans, 1983).

16 Eberhard Jüngel, "Der Alte Mensch—als Kriterium der Lebensqualität: Bemerkungen zur Menschenwürde der Leistungsfähigen Person," in *Entsprechungen: Gott—Wahrheit—Mensch* (Munich: Kaiser, 1980), 318.

17 Eberhard Jüngel, "On Becoming Truly Human: The Significance of the Reformation Distinction between Person and Works for the Self-Understanding of Modern Humanity," in *Theological Essays II*, trans. J. Webster (Edinburgh: T&T Clark, 1995), 225. The reference to Descartes is from his *A Discourse on Method* VI, in *The Rationalists*, trans. John Veitch et al., (New York: Anchor Books, 1974), 84.

18 Martin Luther, *Disputation against Scholastic Theology*, LW 31:12.

19 Eberhard Jüngel, *Death: the Riddle and the Mystery*, trans. Iain and Ute Nicol, (Philadelphia: Westminster, 1974).

20 Ibid., 63.

21 A helpful analysis of this difficult dimension in Jüngel's thought can be found in John Webster, "Justification, Analogy and Action: Barth and Jüngel in Luther's Anthropology" *Barth's Moral Theology* (New York: T&T Clark, 1998), 179–214.

22 Ibid., 77–8.

23 Eberhard Jüngel, *Justification: The Heart of the Christian Faith*, trans. Jeffrey Cayzer, (Edinburgh: T&T Clark, 2001), 144–5, italics his.

24 Presumably, the acknowledgement of such a debt would look something like praise or prayer or some other form of "speaking," though Jüngel never really identifies why he chooses speechlessness as his metaphor.

25 Jüngel, *Justification*, 145.

26 Ibid.

27 Jüngel also has a brief but powerful discussion of sin in *God as the Mystery of the World*, trans. Darrel L. Guder (Grand Rapids, MI: Eerdmans, 1983), 225. He uses language reminiscent of Barth's *das Nichtige* (which

I elucidate elsewhere in this chapter) in describing sin as the "intensified empowerment of nothingness" in that it is the power of nothingness that leads to destruction. What sin destroys is human flourishing, which is an integrated relational whole.

28 There is perhaps no more moving, or more interesting, example of this rebellious encounter than that which takes place in David Lynch's TV series *Twin Peaks* between the stern but loving military dad Major Briggs and his rebellious son Bobby. Major Briggs beautifully justifies the need for impetuous adolescent revolt, but later offers his son a most stirring vision of their eventual reunion that both allows for the self-expression of the son, but also promises to relativize the alienation in the context of anticipated reconciliation.

29 Rom. 5.14–17, NRSV.

30 Otto Michel, *Der Brief an die Römer* (Göttingen: Vandenhoeck and Ruprecht, 1978), 188.

31 Robert Jewett, *Romans* (Minneapolis: Fortress, 2007), 377–8.

32 One feature missed by calling sin "rebellion" is the fundamental *irrationality* of sin in Barth's theology. It also downplays the passive, banal, pathetic instances of sin implicit in his notion of sin as sloth.

33 *CD* IV/1, 488.

34 Matthew Rose, *Ethics with Barth: God, Metaphysics, and Morals* (Burlington, VT: Ashgate, 2010), 176.

35 George Hunsinger, *How to Read Karl Barth: The Shape of His Theology* (New York: Oxford University Press, 1991), 156.

36 *CD* IV/2, 271.

37 *CD* IV/1, 14.

38 *CD* IV/1, 67–8.

39 Karl Barth, *Epistle to the Romans*, trans E. Hoskyns (London: Oxford University Press, 1933), 57.

40 James Gustafson, *Ethics from a Theocentric Perspective* (Chicago: University of Chicago Press, 1984), 1:300. I hasten to add here that Gustafson is not discussing Barth at this point.

41 *CD* IV/1, 91.

42 "When in creation God pronounced His wise and omnipotent Yes He also pronounced His wise and omnipotent No . . . He marked off the positive reality of the creature from that which He did not elect and will and therefore did not create. And to that which He denied He allotted the being of non-being, the existence of that which does not exist [*das Wesen des Unwesens, die Existenz des* Nichtexistierenden]." *CD* III/3, 77.

43 *CD* III/3, 77.

44 *CD* IV/1, 410. For a very helpful amplification of this notion, see Hunsinger, *How To Read Karl Barth*, 39–40.

45 *CD* IV/1, 12.

46 *CD* IV/1, 406. "His own most proper being will be his judge."

47 *CD* IV/1, 282. Barth comments on Romans 3.20: "It is the law which Paul does not interpret apart from the gospel, but rather in the gospel itself and therefore authentically . . . It is by this law that there comes the knowledge of sin." *CD* IV/1, 395.

48 *CD* IV/1, 390.
49 Barth's tri-fold schema of sin corresponds to the knowledge of true humanity revealed in the reconciliation of God with man. Understanding sin as pride, sloth, and falsehood corresponds to the knowledge of Jesus Christ who is "1) very God, that is, the God who humbles Himself, and therefore the reconciling God, 2) very man, that is, man exalted and therefore reconciled to God, and 3) in the unity of the two the guarantor and witness of our atonement." *CD* IV/1, 79.
50 Rose, *Ethics with Barth*, 189.
51 *CD* IV/1, 41–2.
52 *CD* IV/1, 143–4.
53 *CD* IV/2, 403.
54 I have developed the taxonomy of commission/omission further in Derek R. Nelson, "Sins of Commission, Sins of Omission: Ricoeur, Girard and the Armenian Genocide" in Ted Peters, Gaymon Bennett, Martinez Hewlett, and Robert John Russell, eds., *The Evolution of Evil* (Göttingen: Vandenhoeck and Ruprecht, 2008), 318–33.
55 *CD* IV/2, 404.
56 *CD* IV/3.1, 470.
57 I should add here that Barth views the three forms of sin as corresponding to negations of the *triplex munus* of Christ; Christ's office as King is controverted in the sin of sloth, his office as Priest in the sin of pride, and his office as prophet (and thus, truth-teller) in the sin of falsehood.
58 *CD* IV/1, 144.
59 *CD* IV/3.1, 368.
60 *CD* IV/3.1, 437.
61 *CD* IV/3.1, 436–7.
62 *CD* IV/2, 411.
63 *CD* IV/1, 434.
64 *CD* IV/1, 483.
65 Karl Barth, *The Christian Life*, trans. Geoffrey Bromiley (Grand Rapids, MI: Eerdmans, 1981), 213, and *CD* III/3, 310.
66 *CD* IV/1, 453.
67 Sin as self-justification and scapegoating is a prominent feature of an excellent book on sin by Ted Peters, *Sin: Radical Evil in Soul and Society* (Grand Rapids, MI: Eerdmans, 1994).
68 My understanding of the "narrative" structure of the self, and its implications for moral selfhood and sin, comes from various works by Paul Ricouer, especially *Oneself as Another*, trans. Kathleen Blamey (Chicago: University of Chicago Press, 1992 113–68; and *Time and Narrative*, 3 vols., trans. Kathleen Blamey and David Pellauer (Chicago: University of Chicago Press, 1984–8), 1:31–51.
69 Here Paul Ricoeur and Alisdair MacIntyre have been extremely influential. See Chapter 5 for a brief look at the implications of Ricoeur's narrative theory for a theological understanding of the self-in-relation and sin. On MacIntyre, see his *After Virtue: A Study in Moral Theory*, 3rd ed. (Notre Dame, IN: University of Notre Dame Press, 1981). There he says, for example, "I can only answer the question, 'What am I to do?' if

I can answer the prior question, 'Of what story or stories do I find myself a part?' " (216).

70 Gen. 3.11–13, NRSV.

71 Along these lines, see Jacob Neusner, *A Theological Commentary to the Midrash: Genesis Rabbah* (Washington, DC: University Press of America, 2001), 2.55–62.

72 Martin Luther, *Luther's Works: Lectures on Genesis 1–5*, ed. Jaroslav Pelikan and Helmut Lehmann (Saint Louis: Concordia, 1958), 1:175.

73 Ted Peters, *God—The World's Future: Systematic Theology for a Postmodern Age*, 2nd ed. (Minneapolis: Fortress, 2000), 170.

74 Most commentators believe Tyndale got this wrong. Azazel seems to refer to the name of a demon in the wilderness into whose hands the scapegoat was cast.

75 This is a basic presupposition of Alexandre Kojève's brilliant interpretation of Hegel, for example. See Alexandre Kojève, *Introduction to the Reading of Hegel: Lectures on the Phenomenology of Spirit*, (Ithaca: Cornell University Press, 1980).

76 René Girard, *I See Satan Fall Like Lightning*, trans. James G. Williams (Maryknoll, NY: Orbis, 2001).

77 Ibid., 10.

78 Though I am discussing Girard primarily in terms of "actual sin," many have seen mimesis as a way of elucidating "original sin"—none better than James Alison, *The Joy of Being Wrong: Original Sin though Easter Eyes* (New York: Crossroad Herder, 1998).

79 Girard, *Things Hidden Since the Foundation of the World* (Stanford, CA: Stanford University Press, 1987), 24.

80 One scholar who has paid careful attention to this problem is John Searle, especially *The Construction of Social Reality* (New York: Free Press, 1995), and "Collective Intentions and Actions," in Jerry Morgan, Philip. R. Cohen, and Martha Pollack, eds., *Intentions in Communication* (Cambridge, MA: MIT Press, 1990), 401–16.

81 I borrow the title of this section from Mardy Grothe, *I Never Metaphor I Didn't Like: A Comprehensive Compilation of History's Greatest Analogies, Metaphors and Similies* (New York: HarperCollins, 2008).

82 George Lakoff and Mark Johnson, *Metaphors We Live By* (Chicago: University of Chicago Press, 1980).

83 Ibid., 8.

CHAPTER 5

1 A fascinating work on Bonhoeffer's poetry as an entry point into his theology has recently appeared from Bernd Wannenwetsch, *Who Am I?: Bonhoeffer's Theology through His Poetry* (New York and London: T&T Clark, 2009).

2 URL: www.catholicnewsagency.com/new.php?n=12031, accessed July 18, 2008.

3 I use the old distinction of "American philosophy" being largely discontinuous from "philosophy done in America." The latter uses imported

thought forms, usually from Continental Europe or Great Britain. For more on the distinction, see the popular account in Cornel West, *The American Evasion of Philosophy* (Madison: University of Wisconsin Press, 1989), or the classic (albeit a bit dated) from Arthur Schlesinger, Jr., *Paths of American Thought* (Boston: Houghton Mifflin, 1963).

4 Representative works are, respectively, *Philosophy and the Mirror of Nature* (Princeton: Princeton University Press, 1979), *Contingency, Irony and Solidarity* (Cambridge: Cambridge University Press, 1989), and *Consequences of Pragmatism* (Minneapolis: University of Minnesota Press, 1982).

5 I explore this view further in Derek R. Nelson, "Inquiry, Conversation and Theistic Belief: William James and Richard Rorty Get Religion," *Heythrop Journal* 50 (2009):3, 495–507.

6 *Consequences of Pragmatism*, xlii, emphasis mine.

7 Ibid.

8 What I mean by "faculty anthropology" is a version of human nature which rests on noting a particular power or trait or set of powers or traits which humans are said to have. The faculty named as the *sine qua non* of human nature has varied greatly in history, though the usual suspects are free will, consciousness, reason, the soul, transcendence, and the conscience. Views of the relational self may employ these conceptions, but usually make the critical distinction that the faculties of a human person are reflective, not constitutive, of personhood.

9 The best introductions to Whitehead's philosophy and its implications for Christian theology are C. Robert Mesle, *Process-Relational Philosophy: An Introduction to Alfred North Whitehead* (West Consohocken, PA: Templeton Foundation Press, 2008) and Delwin Brown, *Process Philosophy and Christian Thought* (Indianapolis: Bobbs Merrill, 1971).

10 The main works we examine here are Marjorie Hewitt Suchocki, *God, Christ, Church: A Practical Guide to Process Theology*, (New York: Crossroad, 1982) and *The Fall to Violence: Original Sin in Relational Theology*, (New York: Continuum, 1994).

11 *God, Christ, Church*, 257.

12 Alfred North Whitehead, *Process and Reality*, ed. David Ray Griffin and Donald W. Sherburne (New York: Free Press, 1978), 21.

13 The difference between an actual occasion and an actual entity is only that God is an actual entity, and never an actual occasion, because God is nontemporal in God's primordial nature, whereas actual occasions are by definition temporal.

14 Whitehead, *Process and Reality*, 151, and passim.

15 This has implications for Ricoeur's distinction between ipse identity and idem identity, as I will discuss later. I wish Ricoeur discussed Whitehead extensively somewhere; apart from a few sparse allusions, as far as I know, he does not.

16 Suchocki, *God, Christ, Church*, 17.

17 Ibid.

18 Suchocki, *The Fall to Violence*, 126, italics hers.

19 Suchocki, *God, Christ, Church*, 18.

20 Ibid., 20.

21 Ibid., 21.

22 Suchocki, *The Fall to Violence*, 55.

23 Ibid., 36–8.

24 Ibid., 39–40.

25 Ibid., 40–2.

26 There are some affinities between Suchocki and René Girard on this point.

27 Suchocki, *The Fall to Violence*, 13, 18–19.

28 I have avoided much of the discussion of Suchocki's more doctrinal arguments about the concept of sin not because they are unimportant or uninteresting, but because they have no parallels in Ricoeur and Løgstrup, and therefore would escape comparison.

29 William A. Christian, *An Interpretation of Whitehead's Metaphysics* (New Haven: Yale University Press, 1959), 22, italics his. I should note, however, that while he raises this as a potential objection to the logic of concrescence, he concludes that it does not make the theory internally inconsistent. See ibid., 42–7. I believe that the objection does significantly vitiate process-based anthropologies, though perhaps not process metaphysics in general.

30 Suchocki, *God, Christ, Church*, 17.

31 Suchocki, *The Fall to Violence*, 134.

32 Ibid., 132.

33 Knud Løgstrup, *Den Etiske Fordring* (Copenhagen: Gyldendals Forlag, 1966), Trans.Theodor I. Jenson, with a foreword by James Gustafson, (Philadelphia: Fortress, 1971).

34 Theologically speaking, Løgstrup considered himself to be a part of the existentialist wing of the dialectical school. He did not study with Bultmann and appears not to have shared the strongly textual interests of the Bultmannian wing of that group. He did, however, find a theological ally in Friedrich Gogarten. In his wonderfully suggestive book *Die Verkündigung Jesu Christi*, Gogarten argued on theological grounds that the relation of the Christian person to God was thoroughly determined by the relation to one's neighbor.

35 A fascinating collection of his correspondence with Danish theologian Hal Koch from this time is published posthumously as *Kære Hal. Kære Koste* (Copenhagen: Gyldendals Forlag, 1992).

36 Ibid., 15.

37 Ibid., 18.

38 Lars-Olle Armgard, "Universal and Specifically Christian Elements in the Writings of K. E. Løgstrup," in Henry Vander Groot, ed., *Creation and Method: Critical Essays on Christocentric Theology* (Washington, DC: University Press of America, 1981), 32.

39 Løgstrup, *The Ethical Demand*, 23.

40 Ibid., 58.

41 Ibid., 61.

42 Gene Outka, *Agape: An Ethical Analysis* (New Haven: Yale University Press, 1972), 275.

43 Løgstrup, *The Ethical Demand*, 219–30, especially at 223–4. This conclusion rests on a persuasive and insightful analysis of forgiveness; were the demand not binding, forgiveness would not be possible, and were it not unfulfillable, forgiveness would be meaningless.

44 Ibid., 44.

45 Levinas was in fact a professor at the University of Strasbourg in 1930 when Løgstrup was a student there, but there is no proof that Løgstrup attended his classes or read his works.

46 Zygmunt Bauman, *Life in Fragments: Essays in Postmodern Morality* (Oxford: Blackwell, 1995), 49–71.

47 Ibid., 60. The cited text is from Emmanuel Levinas, *Entre-Nous: Essais sur le penser-à-l'autre* (Paris: Gasset, 1991), 10, my translation.

48 Hans Fink and Alasdair MacIntyre, "Introduction," in Knud Løgstrup, *The Ethical Demand*, eds. Hans Fink and Alasdair MacIntyre, (Notre Dame, IN: University of Notre Dame Press, 1997), xxxiv. They actually cite three features, of which the second, a political intuition, is not immediately relevant here.

49 See, for example, his *Totality and Infinity: An Essay on Exteriority*, trans. Alphonso Lingis (Pittsburgh: Dusquesne University Press, 1969), 42–7.

50 Løgstrup, *The Ethical Demand*, trans. Jenson, 19 n. 6.

51 Ibid.

52 Ibid., 123.

53 I am grateful for several private conversations on this point with Niels Henrik Gregersen, perhaps the world's most knowledgeable expert on Løgstrup, and the founder of the Løgstrup archives in Aarhus.

54 Paul Ricoeur, *Freud and Philosophy: An Essay on Interpretation*, trans. Denis Savage (New Haven: Yale University Press, 1970).

55 I do not want to make too much of this distinction. Ricoeur never disavowed his early philosophical anthropology, but rather saw his hermeneutics to be a development, not a repudiation, of the philosophy of the will and personalist existentialism.

56 Paul Ricoeur, *Oneself as Another*, trans. Kathleen Blamey (Chicago: University of Chicago Press, 1992). If space permitted, it would be interesting to pair this with the representative work on moral culpability from his philosophy of will, *Fallible Man*.

57 Ibid., 16.

58 Ibid., translation altered.

59 Peter Strawson, *Individuals: An Essay in Descriptive Metaphysics* (London: Methuen, 1959), esp. chapters 1–2.

60 Ricoeur, *Oneself as Another*, 118.

61 Ibid., 119.

62 Ricoeur, *Freedom and Nature:* The *Voluntary and the Involuntary*, trans. Erazim V. Kohák (Evanston, IL: Northwestern University Press, 1966), 355–73.

63 Ricoeur, *Fallible Man*, trans. Charles Kelbley (Chicago: Henry Regnery, 1965), 73–98.

64 Ricoeur, *Oneself as Another*, 119.

65 Ibid., 124.

66 Ricoeur, *Time and Narrative*, 3 vols., trans. Kathleen McLaughlin and David Pellauer (Chicago: University of Chicago Press, 1984–8), esp. 1:52–87.
67 Ricoeur, *Time and Narrative*, 3:158.
68 Ricoeur, *Oneself as Another*, 289 n. 18.
69 Ibid., 350.
70 Ibid., 315.
71 Ibid., 172.
72 Ibid., 193.
73 Ibid., 326.
74 Bernhard Dauenhauer, "Paul Ricoeur," in *The Stanford Encyclopedia of Philosophy*, online version (http://plato.stanford.edu/entries/ricoeur/), accessed November 9, 2010.

CHAPTER 6

1 One helpful way of putting this is found in Paul Tillich, *Systematic Theology*, 2.44–7.
2 Here the technical distinction between "originating original sin" and "originated original sin" (*peccatum originale originans* and *peccatum originale originatum*) is helpful; the first is what Adam did, and is an act. The second is our experience thereof, which is a state.
3 On the "against-ness" of sin, see Chapter 1 above.
4 See Derek R. Nelson, "Schleiermacher and Ritschl on Individual and Social Sin" in *Neue Zeitschrift fuer Theologiegeschicte* 16:2 (2009), 131–54.
5 Walter Rauschenbusch, *A Theology for the Social Gospel* (Nashville: Abingon, 1978). On this see also the perceptive essay of Mark David Chapman, "The *Kingdom of God* and *Ethics*: From *Ritschl* to Liberation Theology" in Robin Barbour, ed., *The Kingdom of God and Human Society* (Edinburgh: T&T Clark, 1993), 140–63; and Gary Dorrien, *Social Ethics in the Making: Interpreting an American Tradition* (Oxford: Blackwell, 2011), 60–108.
6 Gustavo Gutiérrez, "Toward a Theology of Liberation," trans. Jeffrey Klaiber, SJ, in Alfred Hennelly, SJ, ed., *Liberation History: A Documentary History* (Maryknoll, NY: Orbis Books, 1990), 62–76.
7 Gutiérrez, *The Power of the Poor in History*, trans. Robert B. Barr (Maryknoll, NY: Orbis, 1983), 147.
8 Gutiérrez, *The Truth Shall Make You Free: Confrontations*, trans. Matthew J. O'Connell (Maryknoll, NY: Orbis, 1990), 136. Medellín refers to the site of an important theological conference in Colombia in 1968 where many important positions in liberation theology were developed.
9 I have tried to make this case in my book *What's Wrong with Sin: Sin in Individual and Social Perspective from Schleiermacher to Theologies of Liberation* (London: T&T Clark, 2009), especially Chapter 4.
10 *The Truth Shall Make You Free*, 138. The time to which he refers is basically the whole of Christian theological reflection, but particularly the setting of the Medellín and Puebla Latin American bishop's conferences.

11 Ibid.

12 Gutiérrez, *A Theology of Liberation: History, Politics, Salvation*, trans. Sister Caridad Inda and John Eagleson (Maryknoll, NY: Orbis, 1973), 3–12.

13 *Puebla Final Document*, par. 328, in Hennelly, *Liberation Theology: A Documentary History*, 242–58, emphasis added.

14 Gutiérrez, "Freedom as Gift and Task at Puebla," in James B. Nickoloff, ed., *Gustavo Gutiérrez: Essential Writings* (Minneapolis: Fortress Press, 1996), 158.

15 Gutiérrez, *A Theology of Liberation*, 24.

16 Gutiérrez, *Truth Shall Make You Free*, 137–8.

17 Ibid., 139.

18 The revised version of *A Theology of Liberation* contains a fascinating footnote to this effect. Gutiérrez writes, "Sin is a rejection of friendship with God, and *in consequence*, with other human beings. It is a personal free act by which we refuse to accept the gift of God's love" (226 n.101). This is not included in the original version of the book, and could be evidence that Gutiérrez tried to distance himself from the massive shift occurring later in some liberation theologies, in which sin is against God only in view of its violation of neighbor or creation. For more on what is at stake in this distinction, see Gutiérrez, *We Drink from Our Own Wells: The Spiritual Journey of a People*, trans. Matthew J. O'Connell (Maryknoll, NY: Orbis, 1984), 96–9.

19 Gutiérrez, *The Power of the Poor*, 146. The text he cites is from Puebla § 327.

20 Gutiérrez and other liberationists often credit Pope Paul VI's encyclical *Populorum Progressio* for this insight.

21 Gutiérrez, *A Theology of Liberation*, xxxviii.

22 Gutiérrez, *The Truth Shall Make You Free*, 139.

23 See, for example, Michael Sievernich, *Schuld und Sünde in der Theologie der Gegenwart* (Frankfurt: Knecht, 1982), 265–8, for an assessment of the German-language reaction to this distinction. *Mujerista* theology developed partially due to the realization that the sin of sexism was often hidden under claims to innocence by "oppressed" Latin American men. One of the most articulate, even if sometimes intransigent, critics of the rigidification of the oppressor/oppressed distinction is Schubert Ogden. See his *Faith and Freedom: Toward a Theology of Liberation* (Nashville: Abingdon, 1979), and his "The Concept of a Theology of Liberation: Must a Christian Theology Today Be So Conceived?" in Brian Mahan and L. Dale Richesin, eds., *The Challenge of Liberation Theology: A First World Response* (Maryknoll, NY: Orbis, 1981), 127–40.

24 Valerie Saiving, "The Human Situation: A Feminine View," *Journal of Religion* 40 (1960): 100–12. Saiving also criticizes the Swedish theologian Anders Nygren's anthropology in this essay. I find her objections to Niebuhr far more convincing.

25 Judith Plaskow, *Sex, Sin and Grace: Women's Experience and the Theologies of Reinhold Niebuhr and Paul Tillich* (Lanham, MD: University Press of America, 1980).

26 Susan Nelson Dunfee, "The Sin of Hiding," *Soundings* 65 (1982): 316–27.
27 Daphne Hampson, "Reinhold Niebuhr on Sin: A Critique," in *Reinhold Niebuhr and the Issues of Our Time*, ed. Richard Harries (London: Mowbray, 1986), and idem, "Luther on the Self: A Feminist Critique," in *Feminist Theology: A Reader* (Louisville: Westminster John Knox, 1990), 215–25. The appellation "Christian" is now inappropriate for Hampson, but "theologian" may well not be.
28 New York: Crossroad, 1983.
29 Elisabeth Schüssler Fiorenza, *Bread, Not Stone—The Challenge of Feminist Biblical Interpretation* (Boston: Beacon, 1984).
30 Relevant biblical texts cited by Schüssler Fiorenza would include the fact that women were the first witnesses of the resurrection, that women remained loyal to Jesus during his arrest and trial, and the extreme importance of women as the first followers of Jesus to bring his gospel to a predominantly Gentile audience.
31 Lucia Scherzberg, in her excellent book *Sünde und Gnade in der Feministischen Theologie* (Mainz: Matthias Grünewald, 1991), titles her chapter on Schüssler Fiorenza "Sexism as Structural Sin and the Discipleship of Equals as the Location of the Experience of God," 76–90. However, it is not at all clear that Schüssler Fiorenza objects to such distorted arrangements of power on the grounds that they are *sinful*, which is a theological category with which she seems uncomfortable.
32 Schüssler Fiorenza, *But She Said: Feminist Practices of Biblical Interpretation* (Boston: Beacon Press, 1992) contains the fullest (and first) discussion of *kyriarchy*. For a shorter discussion, see "The Ties that Bind: Domestic Violence against Women," in Mary John Manzanan et al., eds., *Women Resisting Violence: Spirituality for Life* (Maryknoll, NY: Orbis, 1996), 42–6.
33 Schüssler Fiorenza, *In Memory of Her*, xix.
34 This is Schüssler Fiorenza's later word to describe the interpenetrating nature of *kyriarchy* and androcentrism.
35 That is, economic, judicial, educational, and so forth.
36 Schüssler Fiorenza, *In Memory of Her*, 345–6.
37 Schüssler Fiorenza, "Das Schweigen brechen sichtbar werden," in *Concilium* 21 (1985): 388–9; *In Memory of Her*, 347; and "Emanzipation aus der Bibel: Gegen patriarchalisches Christentum," in *Evangelisches Kommentar* 16 (1983): 195–6.
38 Not many feminists have made what seems to me to be the obvious corollary point here; patriarchy and domination is harmful for, and diminishes the flourishing of, men, too, though certainly in different ways than for women. The reasons for this omission are certainly understandable. But the point that in sinful social structures *no one* wins is important enough to make more forcefully.
39 Ivone Gebara, *Out of the Depths: Women's Experience of Evil and Salvation*, trans. Ann Patrick Ware (Minneapolis: Fortress, 2002).
40 Gebara, *Out of the Depths*, 57.
41 It is one that is explicitly indebted to Paul Ricoeur and implicitly to Edmund Husserl.

42 *Out of the Depths*, 11 and 56.
43 Ibid., 42.
44 Ibid.
45 Ibid., 14.
46 Ibid., 4.
47 Ivone Gebara, *Longing for Running Water: Ecofeminism and Liberation*, trans. David Molineaux (Minneapolis: Fortress, 1999).
48 Zygmunt Bauman, *Postmodern Ethics* (Oxford: Blackwell, 1993), 227–8, quoted in Gebara, *Out of the Depths*, 95.
49 Gebara, *Out of the Depths*, 96.
50 Ibid., 98.
51 Ibid., 99.
52 For some moving examples of these, see *Out of the Depths*, 121–32.
53 Gebara, "Option for the Poor as an Option for Poor Women," in Elisabeth Schüssler Fiorenza, ed., *The Power of Naming: A* Concilium *Reader in Feminist Liberation Theology* (Maryknoll, NY: Orbis, 1996), 145.

CONCLUSION

1 A useful introduction to Christian doctrines of human nature can be found in Marc Cortez, *Theological Anthropology: A Guide for the Perplexed* (London: T&T Clark, 2010).
2 See Ted Peters, *God—The World's Future: Systematic Theology for a Post-Modern Age* (Minneapolis: Fortress Press, 2000), 147–50.
3 See Appolodorus, *The Library of Greek Mythology*, trans. and ed., Robin Hard (Oxford: Oxford University Press, 1997), 37–9.
4 Walter A. Elwell and Philip W. Comfort, eds., *The Tyndale Bible Dictionary* (Wheaton, IL: Tyndale House Publishers, 2001), 331.
5 Thomas Aquinas, Ia q.93 a.2.
6 Augustine, *de Gen. ad litt.*, 6.22; Clement of Alexandria, *The Instructor* 3.7; Basil the Great, *Hexameron* 9.2; Gregory of Nyssa, *On the Making of Man* 7.
7 William C. Placher and David Willis-Watkins, *Belonging to God: A Commentary on* A Brief Statement of Faith (Louisville, KY: Westminster John Knox, 1992), 111–12.

BIBLIOGRAPHY

Adams, Marilyn McCord. *Christ and Horrors: The Coherence of Christology.* Cambridge: Cambridge University Press, 2006.

——. *Horrendous Evils and the Goodness of God.* Ithaca: Cornell University Press, 2000.

Alfaro, Juan. *Christian Liberation and Sin.* San Antonio: Mexican American Cultural Center, 1975.

Alison, James. *The Joy of Being Wrong: Original Sin through Easter Eyes.* New York: Crossroad Herder, 1998.

——. *Raising Abel: The Recovery of the Eschatological Imagination.* New York: Crossroad, 1996.

Allen, Leslie, ed. *Darrow and Bryan at Dayton.* New York: A. Lee and Company, 1925.

Althaus, Paul. *The Theology of Martin Luther.* Trans. Robert C. Schulz. Philadelphia: Fortress, 1966.

Anderson, Gary. *Sin: A History.* New Haven: Yale University Press, 2009.

Appolodorus. *The Library of Greek Mythology.* Trans. and ed., Robin Hard. Oxford: Oxford University Press, 1997.

Arendt, Hannah. *The Human Condition.* Chicago: University of Chicago, 1958.

Armgard, Lars-Olle. "Universal and Specifically Christian Elements in the Writings of K. E. Løgstrup." In Henry Vander Groot, ed., *Creation and Method: Critical Essays on Christocentric Theology.* Washington, DC: University Press of America, 1981.

Arsenio, William F., and Elizabeth A. Lemerise, eds. *Emotions, Aggression and Morality in Children: Bridging Development and Psychopathology.* Washington, DC: American Psychological Association, 2010.

Babcock, William S. "Augustine on Sin and Moral Agency." *Journal of Religious Ethics* 16, no. 1 (1988).

Barth, Karl. *The Christian Life.* Trans. Geoffrey Bromiley. Grand Rapids, MI: Eerdmans, 1981.

——. *Church Dogmatics,* 14 vols. Ed. T. F. Torrance and Geoffrey Bromiley. Edinburgh: T&T Clark, 1936–77.

——. *Deliverance to the Captives.* New York: Harper, 1961.

——. *Epistle to the Romans.* Trans E. Hoskyns. London: Oxford University Press, 1933.

——. *Protestant Thought from Rousseau to Ritschl.* Trans. Brian Cozens. New York: Harper and Row, 1959.

Baum, Gregory. "Structures of Sin." In *idem* and Robert Ellsberg, eds., *The Logic of Solidarity: Commentaries on Pope John Paul II's Encyclical* On Social Concern. Maryknoll: Orbis, 1989.

Bauman, Whitney. *Theology, Creation and Environmental Ethics: From* Creatio Ex Nihilo *to* Terra Nullius. New York: Routledge, 2009.

Bauman, Zygmunt. *Life in Fragments: Essays in Postmodern Morality.* Oxford: Blackwell, 1995.

Boda, Mark J. *A Severe Mercy: Sin and Its Remedy in the Old Testament.* Winona Lake, IN: Eisenbrauns, 2009.

Boff, Leonardo. *Liberating Grace.* Trans. John Drury. Maryknoll: Orbis, 1988.

Bonhoeffer, Dietrich. *Creation and Fall: A Theological Exposition of Genesis 1–3.* Trans. Douglas Stephen Bax. Minneapolis: Fortress, 1997.

—. *Schöpfung und Fall: Theologische Auslegung von Genesis 1 bis 3.* München: Christian Kaiser, 1958.

Bonner, Gerald. *St. Augustine of Hippo: Life and Controversies.* Philadelphia: Westminster Press, 1963.

Botterweck, G. Johannes, Helmer Ringgren, and Heinz-Josef Fabry, eds. *Theological Dictionary of the Old Testament.* Grand Rapids: Eerdmans, 1999.

Bouwsma, William. *John Calvin: A Sixteenth Century Portrait.* New York: Oxford University Press, 1989.

Brett, Stephen F. *Slavery and the Catholic Tradition: Rights in the Balance.* New York: Peter Lang, 1994.

Brown, Delwin. *Process Philosophy and Christian Thought.* Indianapolis: Bobbs Merrill, 1971.

Brown, Peter. *Augustine of Hippo.* Berkeley: University of California Press, 1967.

—. *The Body and Society: Men, Women, and Sexual Renunciation in Early Christianity.* New York: Columbia University Press, 1988.

Brueggemann, Walter. *The Prophetic Imagination*, 2nd ed. Minneapolis: Fortress, 2001.

Brueggemann, Walter, Brian K. Blout, and William C. Placher. *Struggling with Scripture.* Louisville, KY: Westminster John Knox, 2002.

Brunner, Emil. *Der Mensch im Widerspruch: Die christliche Lehre vom wahren und vom wirklichen Menschen.* Zürich: Zwingli Verlag, 1941.

Buechner, Frederick. *Telling the Truth: The Gospel as Tragedy, Comedy and Fairy Tale.* New York: Harper and Row, 1977.

Burghardt, Walter S. J. "All Sin Is Social." *Living Pulpit* 8 (1999), 42–6.

Burns, J. Patout, ed. *Theological Anthropology.* Philadelphia: Fortress Press, 1981.

Cabantous, Alain. *Blasphemy: Impious Speech in the West from the Seventeenth to the Nineteenth Century.* Trans. Eric Rauth. New York: Columbia University Press, 2002.

Calvin, John. *Institutes of the Christian Religion.* Trans. John McNeill. Louisville, KY: Westminster John Knox, 1960.

Capps, Donald. *The Depleted Self: Sin in a Narcissistic Age.* Minneapolis: Fortress Press, 1993.

Chapman, Mark. "The *Kingdom of God and Ethics*: From *Ritschl* to Liberation Theology." In Robin Barbour, ed., *The Kingdom of God and Human Society*. Edinburgh: T&T Clark, 1993, 140–63.

Christian, William A. *An Interpretation of Whitehead's Metaphysics*. New Haven: Yale University Press, 1959.

Coffin, William Sloane. *Credo*. Louisville, KY: Westminster John Knox Press, 2004.

Comblin, Jose. *Retrieving the Human: A Christian Anthropology*. Trans. Robert R. Barr. Maryknoll, NY: Orbis, 1990.

Compier, Don H. *John Calvin's Rhetorical Doctrine of Sin*. New York: Mellen, 2001.

Cone, James. *A Black Theology of Liberation*. Maryknoll, NY: Orbis, 1990.

Connolly, Hugh. *Sin*. London: Continuum, 2001.

Cortez, Marc. *Theological Anthropology: A Guide for the Perplexed*. London: T&T Clark, 2010.

Costas, Orlando E. "Sin and Salvation in Latin America." *Theological Fraternity Bulletin* 3 (1981), 1–16.

Couenhoven, Jesse. "St. Augustine's Doctrine of Original Sin." *Augustinian Studies* 36:2 (2005), 359–96.

Dauenhauer, Bernhard. "Paul Ricoeur," in *The Stanford Encyclopedia of Philosophy*, online version (http://plato.stanford.edu/entries/ricoeur/), accessed November 9, 2010.

Dawkins, Richard. *The God Delusion*. New York: Houghton Mifflin, 2006.

Dean, Eric. *The Good News about Sin: Sermons Preached in the Wabash College Chapel*. Crawfordsville, IN: Wabash College, 1982.

Delbanco, Andrew. *The Death of Satan: How Americans Have Lost the Sense of Evil*. New York: Farrar, Straus and Giroux, 1995.

Descartes. *A Discourse on Method* VI, in *The Rationalists*. Trans. John Veitch, et al. New York: Anchor Books, 1974.

Donfried, Karl. "Paul and the Revisionists: Did Luther Really Get Paul Wrong?" *Dialog: A Journal of Theology* 46:1 (2007), 31–40.

Dorrien, Gary. *Social Ethics in the Making: Interpreting an American Tradition*. Oxford: Blackwell, 2011.

Dunfee, Susan Nelson. "The Sin of Hiding: A Feminist Critique of Reinhold Niebuhr's Account of the Sin of Pride,." *Soundings* 65 (1982), 316–27.

Dunn, James D. G. *The Theology of Paul the Apostle*. Grand Rapids: Eerdmans, 1998.

Edwards, Jonathan. *Original Sin*. New Haven: Yale University Press, 1970.

Eichrodt, Walther. *Theology of the Old Testament*. Trans. John Baker. Philadelphia: Fortress, 1967.

Elliot, Charles. "Structures, Sin and Personal Holiness." In Haddon Willmer, ed., *Christian Faith and Political Hopes*. London, Epworth, 1979.

Elwell, Walter A., ed. *Baker Theological Dictionary of the Bible*. Grand Rapids: Baker Books, 2001.

Elwell, Walter A. and Philip W. Comfort, eds. *The Tyndale Bible Dictionary*. Wheaton, IL: Tyndale House Publishers, 2001.

Engberg-Pedersen, Troels. *Paul and the Stoics.* Louisville, KY: Westminster John Knox, 2000.

Engel, Mary Potter. "Evil, Sin, and the Violation of the Vulnerable." In *idem* and Susan Brooks Thistlethwaite, eds., *Lift Every Voice: Constructing Christian Theologies from the Underside.* San Francisco: Harper, 1990, 152–64.

—. *John Calvin's Perspectival Anthropology.* Eugene: Wipf and Stock, 2002.

Eslinger, Lyle. "A Contextual Identification of the bene ha'elohim and benoth ha'adam in Genesis 6:1–4." *Journal for the Study of the Old Testament* 13 (July 1979), 65–73.

Etchegoyen, Aldo. "Theology of Sin and Structures of Oppression." In Dow Kirkpatrick, ed., *Faith Born in the Struggle for Life: A Reading of Protestant Faith in Latin America Today.* Grand Rapids: Eerdmans, 1988.

Farley, Edward. *Good and Evil: Interpreting a Human Condition.* Minneapolis: Fortress, 1990.

Fink, Hans, and Alasdair MacIntyre. "Introduction." In Knud Løgstrup, *The Ethical Demand.* Eds. Hans Fink and Alasdair MacIntyre. Notre Dame: University of Notre Dame Press, 1997.

Flaherty, Wendy Doniger. *The Origins of Evil in Hindu Mythology.* Berkeley: University of California Press, 1976.

Ford, David. *Self and Salvation: Being Transformed.* Cambridge: Cambridge University Press, 1999.

Fredrickson, David E. "Ephesians and Stoic Physics." *Word and World* 22:2 (2002), 144–54.

Freedman, David. *Anchor Bible Dictionary.* New Haven, CT: Yale University Press, 1992.

Furnish, Victor Paul. *Theology and Ethics in Paul,* rev. ed. Louisville, KY: Westminster John Knox, 2009.

Gebara, Ivonne. *Longing for Running Water: Ecofeminism and Liberation.* Trans. David Molineaux. Minneapolis: Fortress, 1999.

—. "Option for the Poor as an Option for Poor Women." In Elisabeth Schüssler Fiorenza, ed., *The Power of Naming: A* Concilium *Reader in Feminist Liberation Theology.* Maryknoll: Orbis, 1996.

—. *Out of the Depths: Women's Experience of Evil and Salvation.* Trans. Ann Patrick Ware. Minneapolis: Fortress, 2002.

Gerrish, B. A. *Grace and Gratitude: The Eucharistic Theology of John Calvin.* Minneapolis: Fortress, 1993.

—. "The Mirror of God's Goodness: Man in the Theology of John Calvin." *Concordia Theological Quarterly* 45:3 (1981), 211–22.

Gestrich, Christof. *Peccatum—Studien zur Sündenlehre.* Tübingen: Mohr Siebeck, 2003.

Girard, René. *I See Satan Fall Like Lightning.* Trans. James G. Williams. Maryknoll: Orbis, 2001.

—. *The Scapegoat.* Trans. Yvonne Frecerro. Baltimore: Johns Hopkins University Press, 1986.

—. *Things Hidden since the Foundation of the World.* Trans. Stephen Bann. Stanford, CA: Stanford University Press, 1987.

Glucklich, Ariel. *Sacred Pain: Hurting the Body for the Sake of the Soul.* New York: Oxford University Press, 2001.

Gonzalez, Justo. "The Alienation of Alienation." In Andrew Sung Park and Susan L. Nelson, eds., *The Other Side of Sin: Woundedness from the Perspective of the Sinned-Against.* Albany: SUNY Press, 2001.

Goodman Kaufman, Carol. *Sins of Omission: The Jewish Community's Reaction to Domestic Violence.* Boulder: Westview, 2003.

Grant, Jacqueline. "The Sin of Servanthood: And the Deliverance of Discipleship." In Emilie Townes, ed., *A Troubling in My Soul: Womanist Perspectives on Evil and Suffering.* Maryknoll: Orbis, 1993, 199–218.

Grothe, Mardy. *I Never Metaphor I Didn't Like: A Comprehensive Compilation of History's Greatest Analogies, Metaphors and Similies.* New York: HarperCollins, 2008.

Gudorf, Christine. "Admonishing the Sinner: Owning Structural Sin." In Francis A. Eigo, ed., *Rethinking the Spiritual Works of Mercy.* Villanova: Villanova University Press, 1983.

Gustafson, James. *Ethics from a Theocentric Perspective*, 2 vols. Chicago: University of Chicago Press, 1981–4.

Gutiérrez, Gustavo. "Freedom as Gift and Task at Puebla." In James B. Nickoloff, ed., *Gustavo Gutiérrez: Essential Writings.* Minneapolis: Fortress Press, 1996. Maryknoll, NY: Orbis, 1973.

—. *The Power of the Poor in History.* Trans. Robert B. Barr. Maryknoll, NY: Orbis, 1983.

—. *A Theology of Liberation: History, Politics, Salvation.* Trans. Sister Caridad Inda and John Eagleson. Maryknoll, NY: Orbis, 1973.*The Truth Shall Make You Free: Confrontations.* Trans. Matthew J. O'Connell. Maryknoll, NY: Orbis, 1990.

—. "Toward a Theology of Liberation." Trans. Jeffrey Klaiber, SJ. In Alfred Hennelly, SJ, ed., *Liberation History: A Documentary History.* Maryknoll, NY: Orbis Books, 1990.

—. *We Drink from Our Own Wells: The Spiritual Journey of a People.* Trans. Matthew J. O'Connell. Maryknoll, NY: Orbis, 1984.

Hallo, William W. "Biblical Abominations and Sumerian Taboos." *Jewish Quarterly Review* 76 (1985), 21–40.

Hampson, Daphne. "Luther on the Self: A Feminist Critique." In *Feminist Theology: A Reader.* Louisville, KY: Westminster John Knox, 1990, 215–25.

—. "Reinhold Niebuhr on Sin: A Critique." In Richard Harries, ed., *Reinhold Niebuhr and the Issues of Our Time.* London: Mowbray, 1986. Louisville, KY.

Häring, Bernhard. *The Law of Christ: Moral Theology for Priests and Laity.* Trans. Edwin G. Kaiser. 3 vols. Westminster, MD: Newman, 1961.

—. *Sünde im Zeitalter der Säkularisation.* Graz: Verlag Styria, 1974.

Hauerwas, Stanley. *Truthfulness and Tragedy: Further Investigations into Christian Ethics.* Notre Dame: Notre Dame University Press, 1977.

Hefner, Philip. *The Human Factor: Evolution, Culture and Religion.* Minneapolis: Fortress Press, 1993.

Heidegger, Martin. *Being and Time.* Trans. Joan Stambaugh. Albany: SUNY Press, 1996.

Henriot, Peter. "Social Sin: The Recovery of a Christian Tradition." In James D. Whitehead, ed., *Method in Ministry.* New York: Seabury, 1980.

Hick, John. *Evil and the God of Love.* London: Macmillan, 1960.

Himes, Kenneth. "Social Sin and the Role of the Individual." *Annual of the Society* 6 (1986), 183–218.

Hunsinger, George. *How to Read Karl Barth: The Shape of His Theology.* New York: Oxford University Press, 1991.

Hyers, Conrad. *The Meaning of Creation: Genesis and Modern Science.* Louisville, KY: Westminster John Knox, 1984.

Jacobs, Alan. *Original Sin: A Cultural History.* New York: HarperOne, 2008.

James, William. *The Varieties of Religious Experience.* New York: Penguin, 1985.

Jeremias, Joachim. *Jerusalem in the Time of Jesus.* Philadelphia: Fortress, 1969.

——. *New Testament Theology: The Proclamation of Jesus.* New York: Scribners, 1971.

Jewett, Robert. *Romans.* Minneapolis: Fortress, 2007.

Joest, Wilfried. *Ontologie der Person bei Luther.* Göttingen: Vandenhoeck and Ruprecht, 1967.

Jones, Serene. "Bounded Openness: Postmodernism, Feminism and the Church Today." *Interpretation* 55 (2001), 49–59.

Jüngel, Eberhard. *Death—The Riddle and the Mystery.* Trans. Iain and Ute Nicol. Philadelphia: Westminster, 1974.

——. *Entsprechungen: Gott—Wahrheit—Mensch.* Munich: Kaiser, 1980.

——. *God as the Mystery of the World.* Trans. Darrel L. Guder. Grand Rapids: Eerdmans, 1983.

——. *Justification: The Heart of the Christian Faith.* Trans. Jeffrey Cayzer. Edinburgh: T&T Clark, 2001.

——. "On Becoming Truly Human: The Significance of the Reformation Distinction between Person and Works for the Self-Understanding of Modern Humanity." In *Theological Essays II*, trans. J. Webster. Edinburgh: T&T Clark, 1995.

Kelsey, David. *Imagining Redemption.* Louisville, KY: Westminster John Knox Press, 2005.

——. "Whatever Happened to the Doctrine of Sin?" *Theology Today* 50 (1993), 169–78.

Kepnes, Steven. "'Turn Us to You and We Shall Return': Original Sin, Atonement, and Redemption in Jewish Terms." In David Novak et al., ed., *Christianity in Jewish Terms.* Boulder, CO: Westview, 2000.

Kierkegaard, Søren. *The Concept of Anxiety.* Trans. Reidar Thomte. Princeton: Princeton University Press, 1980.

——. *Fear and Trembling.* Trans. Howard and Edna Hong. Princeton, NJ: Princeton University Press, 1983.

——. *The Sickness unto Death.* Trans. Alastair Hannay. London: Penguin, 1989.

Klawens, Jonathan. *Impurity and Sin in Ancient Judaism*. New York: Oxford University Press, 2000.

Koch, Hal. *Kære Hal. Kære Koste*. Copenhagen: Gyldendals Forlag, 1992.

Kojève, Alexandre. *Introduction to the Reading of Hegel: Lectures on the Phenomenology of Spirit*. Ithaca: Cornell University Press, 1980.

Kvam, Kris, et al., eds. *Eve and Adam: Jewish, Christian and Muslim Readings on Genesis and Gender*. Bloomington: Indiana University Press, 1999.

Lakoff, George, and Mark Johnson. *Metaphors We Live By*. Chicago: University of Chicago Press, 1980.

Lane, Belden C. "Spirituality as the Performance of Desire: Calvin's Metaphor of the World as a Theatre of God's Glory." *Spiritus* 1:1 (2001), 1–30.

Levinas, Emmanuel. *Entre-Nous: Essais sur le penser-à-l'autre*. Paris: Gasset, 1991.

—. *Totality and Infinity: An Essay on Exteriority*. Trans. Alphonso Lingis. Pittsburgh: Dusquesne University Press, 1969.

Løgstrup, Knud. *Den Etiske Fordring.* Copenhagen: Gyldendals Forlag, 1966.

—. *The Ethical Demand*. Trans. Theodor I. Jenson, with a foreword by James Gustafson. Philadelphia: Fortress, 1971.

Luther, Martin, Disputation against Scholastic Theology, LW 31:12.

Luther, Martin. *Luther's Works: Lectures on Genesis 1–5*. Ed. Jaroslav Pelikan and Helmut Lehmann. Saint Louis: Concordia, 1958.

MacIntyre, Alisdair. *After Virtue: A Study in Moral Theory,*. South Bend, IN: University of Notre Dame Press, 1984.

McCormick, Patrick. *Sin as Addiction*. New York: Paulist, 1989.

McDermott, Gerald, ed. *Understanding Jonathan Edwards: An Introduction to America's Theologian*. New York: Oxford University Press, 2003.

McFadyen, Alistair. *Bound to Sin: Abuse, Holocaust and the Christian Doctrine of Sin*. Cambridge: Cambridge University Press, 2000.

—. *The Call to Personhood: A Christian Theory of the Individual in Social Relationships*. Cambridge: Cambridge University Press, 1990.

McFarland, Ian A. *Difference and Identity: A Theological Anthropology*. Cleveland: Pilgrim Press, 2001.

McHenry, Henry. "Human Evolution." In Michael Ruse, Joseph Travis, and E. O. Wilson, eds., *Evolution: The First Four Billion Years*. Cambridge, MA: Belknap Press of Harvard University Press, 2005.

Menninger, Karl. *Whatever Became of Sin?* New York: Hawthorn, 1973.

Mesle, C. Robert. *Process-Relational Philosophy: An Introduction to Alfred North Whitehead*. West Consohocken, PA: Templeton Foundation Press, 2008.

Metzger, Bruce M. *An Introduction to the Apocrypha*. New York: Oxford University Press, 1977.

Michel, Otto. *Der Brief an die Römer.* Göttingen: Vandenhoeck and Ruprecht, 1978.

Milbank, John. *Theology and Social Theory.* Oxford: Blackwell, 1990.

Milgrom, Jacob. "The Concept of ma'al in the Bible and the Ancient Near East." *Journal of the American Oriental Society* 96 (1976), 236–47.

Nelson, Derek R. "Inquiry, Conversation and Theistic Belief: William James and Richard Rorty Get Religion." *Heythrop Journal* 50:3 (2009), 495–507.

—. "Schleiermacher and Ritschl on Individual and Social Sin." In *Neue Zeitschrift fuer Theologiegeschicte* 16:2 (2009), 131–54.

—. "Sins of Commission, Sins of Omission: Ricoeur, Girard and the Armenian Genocide." In Ted Peters, Gaymon Bennett, Martinez Hewlett, and Robert John Russell, eds., *The Evolution of Evil*. Göttingen: Vandenhoeck and Ruprecht, 2008, 318–33.

—. *What's Wrong with Sin: Sin in Individual and Social Perspective from Schleiermacher to Theologies of Liberation*. London: T&T Clark, 2009.

Neusner, Jacob. *A Theological Commentary to the Midrash: Genesis Rabbah*. Washington, DC: University Press of America, 2001.

Niebuhr, H. Richard. *The Kingdom of God in America*. New York: Harper and Row, 1937.

Niebuhr, Reinhold. *Man's Nature and His Communities*. New York: Charles Scribner's Sons, 1965.

—. *Moral Man and Immoral Society*. New York: Charles Scribner's Sons, 1932.

—. *The Nature and Destiny of Man*, 2 vols. New York, Charles Scribner's Sons, 1941.

Ogden, Schubert. "The Concept of a Theology of Liberation: Must a Christian Theology Today Be So Conceived?" In Brian Mahan and L. Dale Richesin, eds., *The Challenge of Liberation Theology: A First World Response*. Maryknoll, NY: Orbis, 1981.

—. *Faith and Freedom: Toward a Theology of Liberation*. Nashville: Abingdon, 1979.

O'Keefe, Mark. "Social Sin and Fundamental Option." In Clayton N. Jefford, ed., *Christian Freedom*. New York: Peter Lang, 1993.

—. *What Are They Saying About Social Sin?* New York: Paulist Press, 1990.

O'Neill, Andrew. *Tillich: A Guide for the Perplexed*. London and New York: T&T Clark, 2008.

Outka, Gene. *Agape: An Ethical Analysis*. New Haven: Yale University Press, 1972.

Pagels, Elaine. *Gnostic Paul: Gnostic Exegesis of the Pauline Letters*. Harrisburg: Trinity, 1992.

—. *The Origin of Satan*. New York: Vintage, 1996.

Pannenberg, Wolfhart. *Anthropology in Theological Perspective*. Trans. Matthew J. O'Connell. Louisville, KY: Westminster, 1985.

—. *What is Man?* Trans. Duane A. Priebe. Philadelphia: Fortress, 1970.

Parker, T. H. L. *Calvin's Doctrine of the Knowledge of God*. Grand Rapids, MI: Eerdmans, 1959.

Peters, Ted. *God—The World's Future: Systematic Theology for a Postmodern Age*, 2nd ed. Minneapolis: Fortress, 2000.

—. *Sin: Radical Evil in Soul and Society*. Grand Rapids, MI: Eerdmans, 1994.

Pieper, Josef. *Über den Begriff der Sünde*. München: Kösel, 1977.

Placher, William C. *The Domestication of Transcendence: Where Modern Thinking about God Went Wrong.* Louisville, KY: Westminster John Knox, 1996.

—. *A History of Christian Theology.* Louisville, KY: Westminster John Knox Press, 1983.

Placher, William C and David Willis-Watkins. *Belonging to God: A Commentary on* A Brief Statement of Faith. Louisville, KY: Westminster John Knox, 1992.

Plantinga, Cornelius, Jr. *Not the Way It's Supposed to Be: A Breviary of Sin.* Grand Rapids, MI: Eerdmans, 1995.

Plaskow, Judith. *Sex, Sin and Grace: Women's Experience and the Theologies of Reinhold Niebuhr and Paul Tillich.* Lanham: University Press of America, 1980.

Pope, Alexander. *Essay on Man and Satires.* Middlesex: Echo, 2007.

Portman, John . *A History of Sin: Its Evolution to Today and Beyond.* Lanham, MD: Rowman and Littlefield, 2007.

—. *In Defense of Sin.* New York: Palgrave, 2001.

Puebla Final Document, par. 328, in Hennelly, Liberation Theology: A Documentary History, 242–58.

Ramm, Bernard. *An Offense to Reason: A Theology of Sin.* San Fancisco: Harper and Row, 1986.

Rauschenbusch, Walter. *A Theology for the Social Gospel.* Nashville: Abingdon, 1978.

Ricoeur, Paul. *Fallible Man.* Trans. Charles Kelbley. Chicago: Henry Regnery, 1965.

—. *Freedom and Nature: The Voluntary and the Involuntary.* Trans. Erazim V. Kohák. Evanston: Northwestern University Press, 1966.

—. *Freud and Philosophy: An Essay on Interpretation.* Trans. Denis Savage. New Haven: Yale University Press, 1970.

—. *Oneself as Another.* Trans. Kathleen Blamey. Chicago: University of Chicago Press, 1992.

—. *The Symbolism of Evil.* Trans. Emerson Buchanan. Boston: Beacon, 1986.

—. *Time and Narrative,* 3 vols. Trans. Kathleen McLaughlin and David Pellauer. Chicago: University of Chicago Press, 1984–8.

Ringe, Sharon. *Luke.* Louisville, KY: Westminster John Knox, 1995.

Rombs, Ronnie J. *Saint Augustine and the Fall of the Soul: Beyond O'Connell and His Critics.* Washington, DC: Catholic University Press, 2006.

Rorty, Richard. *Consequences of Pragmatism.* Minneapolis: University of Minnesota Press, 1982.

—. *Contingency, Irony and Solidarity.* Cambridge: Cambridge University Press, 1989.

—. *Philosophy and the Mirror of Nature.* Princeton: Princeton University Press, 1979.

Rose, Matthew. *Ethics with Barth: God, Metaphysics, and Morals.* Burlington: Ashgate, 2010.

Ruether, Rosemary Radford. *Sexism and God-Talk.* Boston: Beacon, 1983.

—. *Women and Redemption: A Theological History.* Minneapolis: Fortress Press, 1998.

—. "Women and Sin: Response to Mary Lowe." *Dialog: A Journal of Theology* 39 (2000), 229–35.

Sagan, Carl. *Contact*. New York: Pocket Books, 1985.

Saiving, Valerie. "The Human Situation: A Feminine View." *Journal of Religion* 40 (1960), 100–12.

Sampley, J. Paul. *Paul in the Greco-Roman World: A Handbook*. New York: Continuum, 2003.

Sanders, E. P. *Paul and Palestinian Judaism*. Minneapolis: Fortress, 1977.

Scherzberg, Lucia. *Sünde und Gnade in der Feministischen Theologie*. Mainz: Matthias Grünewald, 1992.

Schimmel, Solomon. *The Seven Deadly Sins: Jewish, Christian, and Classical Reflections on Human Nature*. New York: Oxford University Press, 1996.

Schlesinger, Arthur, Jr. *Paths of American Thought*. Boston: Houghton Mifflin, 1963.

Schmitals, Walter. *Paul and the Gnostics*. Nashville: Abingdon, 1972.

Schoonenberg, Piet. *Man and Sin: A Theological View*. Trans. Joseph Donceel. Notre Dame: Notre Dame University Press, 1965.

Schüssler Fiorenza, Elisabeth. *Bread, Not Stone—The Challenge of Feminist Biblical Interpretation*. Boston: Beacon, 1984.

—. *But She Said: Feminist Practices of Biblical Interpretation*. Boston: Beacon Press, 1992.

—. Das Schweigen brechen sichtbar warden." *Concilium* 21 (1985), 388–9.

—. "Emanzipation aus der Bibel: Gegen patriarchalisches Christentum." *Evangelisches Kommentar* 16 (1983), 195–6.

—. *In Memory of Her: A Feminist Theological Reconstruction of Christian Origins*. New York: Crossroad, 1983.

—. "The Ties that Bind: Domestic Violence against Women." In Mary John Manzanan, et al., eds., *Women Resisting Violence: Spirituality for Life*. Maryknoll: Orbis, 1996, 42–6.

Scofield, Sandra. *Occasions of Sin*. New York: Norton, 2004.

Searle, John. "Collective Intentions and Actions." In Jerry Morgan, Philip. R. Cohen, and Martha Pollack, eds., *Intentions in Communication*. Cambridge, MA: MIT Press, 1990, 401–16.

—. *The Construction of Social Reality*. New York: Free Press, 1995.

—. *Intentionality: An Essay in the Philosophy of Mind*. Cambridge: Cambridge University Press, 1983.

Shea, John. *What a Modern Catholic Believes about Sin*. Chicago: Thomas More Press, 1971.

Sievernich, Michael. *Schuld und Sünde in der Theologie der Gegenwart*. Frankfurt: Knecht, 1982.

Stendahl, Krister. "The Apostle Paul and the Introspective Conscience of the West." *Harvard Theological Review* 56 (1963), 199–215.

Strawson, Peter. *Individuals: An Essay in Descriptive Metaphysics*. London: Methuen, 1959.

Suchocki, Marjorie. *The Fall to Violence: Original Sin in Relational Theology*. New York: Continuum, 1994.

—. *God, Christ, Church: A Practical Guide to Process Theology.* New York: Crossroad, 1982.

Sudduth, Michael L. Czapkay. "The Prospects for Mediate Natural Theology in John Calvin." *Religious Studies* 31 (1995), 53–68.

Tappert, T. G. ed. and trans. *Luther's Letters of Spiritual Counsel.* Philadelphia: Westminster, 1960.

Taylor, James. *Sin: A New Understanding of Virtue and Vice.* Kelowna, BC: Northstone, 1997.

Taylor, Mark C. *Journeys to Selfhood: Hegel and Kierkegaard.* Berkeley: University of California Press, 1980.

Tentler, Thomas. *Sin and Confession on the Eve of the Reformation.* Princeton, NJ: Princeton University Press, 1977.

Tillich, Paul. *Systematic Theology*, 3 vols. Chicago: University of Chicago Press, 1951–63.

Torrance, Thomas F. *Calvin's Doctrine of Man.* London: Lutterworth, 1949.

van der Toorn, K. *Sin and Sanction in Israel and Mesopotamia: A Comparative Study.* Assen, Netherlands: Van Gorcum, 1985.

Vickers, Jason E. *Wesley: A Guide for the Perplexed.* London: Continuum, 2009.

Volf, Miroslav. *Exclusion and Embrace: A Theological Exploration of Identity, Otherness, and Reconciliation.* Nashville: Abingdon, 1996.

—. "The Lamb of God and the Sin of the World." In David Novak et al., ed., *Christianity in Jewish Terms.* Boulder, CO: Westview, 2000.

Walton, John H., et al., eds. *The IVP Bible Background Commentary.* Downer's Grove, IL: Intervarsity Press, 2000.

Wannenwetsch, Bernd. *Who Am I?: Bonhoeffer's Theology through His Poetry.* New York and London: T&T Clark, 2009.

Webb, Stephen H. *The Divine Voice: Christian Proclamation and the Theology of Sound.* Grand Rapids: Brazos, 2004.

—. Review of James Morone, *Hellfire Nation: The Politics of Sin in American History.* In *Conversations in Religion and Theology* 4:2 (2006).

Weber, Dorothea. "Some Literary Aspects of the Debate between Julian of Eclanum and Augustine." *Studia Patristica* 43 (2006), 289–302.

Webster, John B. *Barth's Moral Theology.* New York: T&T Clark, 1998.

West, Cornel. *The American Evasion of Philosophy.* Madison: University of Wisconsin Press, 1989.

Westphal, Merold. *Hegel, Freedom and Modernity.* Albany, NY: SUNY Press, 1992.

Whitehead, Alfred North. *Process and Reality.* Ed. David Ray Griffin and Donald W. Sherburne. New York: Free Press, 1978.

Wiley, Tatha. *Original Sin: Origins, Developments, Contemporary Meanings.* New York: Paulist, 2002.

Wills, Garry. *Papal Sin: Structures of Deceit.* New York: Doubleday, 2000.

Wilson, Robert R. "Who Was the Deuteronomist? (Who Was Not the Deuteronomist?): Reflections on Pan-Deuteronomism." In Linda Schearing & Steven L. McKenzie, ed., *Those Elusive Deuteronomists: "Pan-Deuteronomism" and Scholarship in the Nineties.* Sheffield: JSOT Press, 1999, 67–82.

Wolterstorff, Nicholas. *Until Justice and Peace Embrace*. Grand Rapids, MI: Eerdmans, 1983.

Yarnold, Edward, S. J. *The Theology of Original Sin*. Hales Corner, WI.: Clergy Book Service, 1971.

Zachmann, Randall. *The Assurance of Faith: Conscience in the Theology of Martin Luther and John Calvin*. Minneapolis: Fortress, 1993.

INDEX OF SCRIPTURE REFERENCES

GENERAL INDEX